Handbook
to a
Happier Life

Handbook to a Happier Life

A SIMPLE GUIDE TO CREATING THE LIFE YOU'VE ALWAYS WANTED

Jim Donovan

NEW WORLD LIBRARY
NOVATO, CALIFORNIA
www.newworldlibrary.com

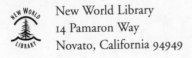

New World Library
14 Pamaron Way
Novato, California 94949

Front cover design by Mary Ann Casler
Text design by Tona Pearce Myers
Typography by Cathey Flickinger

Parts of this book were previously published by Bovan Publishing Group, Inc.

Library of Congress Cataloging-in-Publication Data
Donovan, Jim
    Handbook to a happier life : a simple guide to creating the life you've always wanted / Jim Donovan.
        p.   cm.
Includes bibliographical references.
ISBN 1-57731-401-8 (pbk. : alk. paper)
1. Self-realization. 2. Conduct of life. 3. Happiness. I. Title.
BJ1470 .D66 2003
170'.44—dc21   2002154290

First Printing, April 2003
ISBN 1-57731-401-8
Printed in Canada on partially recycled, acid-free paper
Distributed to the trade by Publishers Group West

10   9   8   7   6   5   4   3   2   1

Dedicated to Georgia, my wife and best friend.
Without her patience, support, and encouragement,
this book would never have been written.

CONTENTS

If you advance confidently in the direction of your dreams,
endeavor to live the life which you've imagined, you will
meet with a success unexpected in common hours.

— Henry David Thoreau

Acknowledgments

I offer my most heartfelt thanks to my mother, Marguerite Donovan, for first teaching me to read and instilling in me a love for the written word. It has been my most cherished gift. And to my mother-in-law, Jean Policastro, for her faith in me and her constant encouragement. I miss them both daily.

To Georgia, my wife and best friend, for all her patience and unconditional support. Without her faith in my abilities, I would not be writing. Heartfelt thanks to Nancy and Terry Sibley for their belief in my books and support for my work.

To Georgia Hughes for championing this book, to

Mimi Kusch, copyeditor, for making it better. To everyone at New World Library who worked to make this book what it is: Mary Ann Casler for the great cover; Cathey Flickinger for the type design and typesetting; and Marjorie Conte for her enthusiastic publicity work.

Most of all, I want to thank the many readers who took the time to write and share their dreams with me. It's their dedication to creating a better life that motivates me to be the best I can be.

I especially want to recognize and thank all the mentors and teachers, too numerous to mention, who have gone before me. Their teachings have enabled me to walk my path and assimilate the knowledge and information I now pass on to you.

Introduction

Welcome to Your Life

This is not a self-improvement book. You are fine, right where you are, doing just what you are doing. You can, however, grow and develop further. This book is intended as a handbook to your personal growth and development.

You are entitled to live a long, joyous, abundant, exciting life. It is your birthright. If you are experiencing less, you are shortchanging yourself. While I cannot provide you with this kind of life, throughout this book I will share with you some of the concepts, techniques, and tools that have helped me and countless others to improve the quality of our lives and to begin reaching our full potential as human beings.

This is not a theoretical treatise. I have used the ideas presented in this book in my own life: I have, as they say, "walked my talk." The techniques I'm sharing with you may be simple, but they are not necessarily easy. Easy things require no effort. Implementing the ideas presented in this book will require some effort, but the result — living a happier life — will be well worth the effort.

QUESTION EVERYTHING

Some of the ideas in this book will be new to you, and some you will be familiar with. Some you will embrace, and some you will reject. Take nothing at face value. If something does not feel right to you, skip over it. Throughout our lives too many people have told us what to do and what to think. The time has come for us to make our own decisions based on what feels right to us.

If something in this book does strike a chord in you, make it yours. Work and play with the concepts presented. Complete the exercises that you will find throughout the book. These exercises are meant to help you make the concepts you encounter more concrete. You may even want to refer back to them from time to time to gauge your progress. Add your own ideas and experiences. Let your imagination run free. Have fun. And above all, be true to yourself.

WHY I WROTE THIS BOOK

As you read through *Handbook to a Happier Life*, you may wonder who I am and how I came to write this book. As I mentioned, I've walked my talk, and perhaps a bit of my story will serve to demonstrate how all the ideas here work.

After many years of living in a downward spiral, I had hit rock bottom. I was spiritually, emotionally, physically, and financially broke. I was out of control. My own family did not even want me around. I had only one friend left who would tolerate my behavior, Charlie Blackmore, but even his patience wore thin. Through the grace of God and help from a lot of people, I was finally able to begin getting my life back on track. During this time of rebuilding my life, I became a student of personal growth and self-help. I read everything I could get my hands on, listened to countless tapes, and attended numerous seminars.

I began applying what I had learned in my own life, and before long, I started seeing results. Wanting to share my newfound knowledge, I began writing. I started with a newsletter, and after several years and a lot of positive encouragement, I wrote *Handbook to a Happier Life*, which I self-published in a previous version. I was overwhelmed by the response to this simple little book. The sales of my book were terrific, and the letters and e-mails I have received have been both gratifying and humbling. After all, who am I to write a book? I'm just an ordinary guy. I don't have impressive educational credentials. Truth be known, I barely finished high school.

One thing I do have, however, is experience. I know the principles in this book work; I am living proof of their effectiveness. I have used the simple ideas in this book to make major changes in my life and continue to use them daily. The fact that I live what I consider to be a dream life today is all the reason I need to keep applying these principles. They have worked for me, and they'll work for you if...you use them! It is now up to you. If you're serious about making your life everything you want it to be, don't just passively read through this book. Apply the ideas you find to your own life. Do the exercises, and keep track of your progress.

When you're ready to take charge of your destiny, turn the page and begin.

1

Happiness

How many times have you said, "All I want is to be happy"? So many of us get caught up in looking outside ourselves for happiness when, in fact, happiness is something that you can choose at any time. The old saying "Happiness is an inside job" does not refer to working indoors. It means that it is we who choose whether or not to be happy.

> *There is no way to happiness.*
> *Happiness is the way.*
> — Wayne Dyer

I chose the title *Handbook to a Happier Life* because that is what it all boils down to. Most of us just want to be happy. A wonderful spiritual study, *A Course in*

1

Miracles, states not only that you should be happy, but also that you should *make* yourself happy. Although this book offers tools to assist you in your quest for happiness, it is important that you realize that, in the end, it is you who holds the key to a happier life.

In any situation, you can choose how you represent what is taking place. You can give away your power and let outside circumstances take away your happiness, or you can claim your God-given birthright to be happy, regardless of what is going on around you. Think about it. How many times have you become unhappy because of something completely out of your control? How many times have you let other people's opinions of you or even the weather control how you feel?

> *Remember:*
> *This is your life,*
> *not a dress rehearsal.*

There was a time in my life when I thought that if I just bought enough "stuff" I would be happy. I thought a new car or a better stereo or bigger house would do the trick. I also used to look to other people to provide the happiness that was lacking in my life. When these methods didn't work and I was still not happy, I would be devastated. I now realize that all the material things and all the people in the world cannot, in and of themselves, make me happy. Only I can.

I wrote this book to help you discover what is preventing you from being happy right now in this moment. You are about to embark on a wonderful journey toward self-discovery. Approach this book with a light heart and a gentle hand, for what you find may surprise and delight you beyond your wildest dreams.

2

The Beginning:
Acceptance

If you want to achieve happiness and live your life to the fullest, the first step is to accept where you are and who you are, right now. This is where change begins.

All too often we look at a situation, decide how we think it should be, and then act on our perception of it. The problem with this approach is that it is based on pure fantasy. If all we do is wish things were different, we will wind up being constantly frustrated. How many people are in relationships that are not working, telling themselves everything is fine when, clearly, it is not? Instead of living in denial, face the reality of what is happening, accept it, and decide do something about it. Perhaps your relationship would benefit from seeking a marriage therapist or maybe something as simple as scheduling special time together.

We must learn to accept circumstances as they are, not as we would like them to be. How many times have you said, "If only it wasn't raining, then I would be happy"? A happy person will accept the rain and go on with her life.

In all my books I always include a short, simple prayer called the Serenity Prayer, which dates back to the fifth century. While its origins are unknown, it was rediscovered by a theologian named Reinhold Niebuhr, who gave it to the founder of Alcoholics Anonymous, because he thought it was a fitting guide for people going through change. This wonderful little prayer reminds us to be more accepting:

> *God grant me the*
> *Serenity to accept the things I cannot change,*
> *Courage to change the things I can,*
> *Wisdom to know the difference.*

You cannot change the fact that it is raining, but you can change how you react to it. It is important to know the difference between these two viewpoints.

We must also learn to accept ourselves as we are in the moment. We sabotage ourselves by saying things like, "If only I had more money" or "If I were ten pounds lighter, then...." We cannot change what is. We can, however, accept everything about ourselves, warts and all, right here and right now. Only then can we begin to make the changes we desire and become the person we are capable of becoming. By accepting ourselves right here and right now, we will be less likely to allow occasional setbacks to divert us from our goals.

Once we have learned to accept ourselves, we can then identify those areas we want to change. For example, if I am fifty pounds overweight and telling myself it's because I have "big bones," I am living in denial. If I am overweight, it's because I probably eat too much and don't exercise. Once I accept the fact that I have a weight challenge, I am empowered to begin taking action to change it. Until I get out of denial, I am stuck. Acceptance is the first step in making any change.

A good exercise to assist you in developing acceptance is to take a personal inventory. This is similar to a grocer who, when she wants to know the state of her business, will take an inventory of the store's contents. She will count and itemize the good, sellable merchandise, then separate out the unsellable merchandise and get rid of it.

We can do the same, metaphorically, to determine our personal state of affairs. Here is an exercise to help you do just that.

EXERCISE

◆

Taking Your Personal Inventory

What physical traits are you less than pleased about?

What steps can you take to become physically fit (exercising, eating better, and so on)?

How are your relationships with your family and loved ones? What would you like to improve about them?

Do you like your job? What do you like about it?

If you don't like your job, what would you really like to do?

What skills do you have?

What are your hobbies?

What activities do you enjoy?

What do you like most about yourself?

What do you like least about yourself?

Don't forget to list the things you like about yourself along with those things you want to change. We have a tendency to list only the "bad" and overlook the good parts of ourselves. We all have attributes we like, and it is important not to forget about these. Sure, there are probably lots of characteristics you would like to change, but give yourself a pat on the back for the parts you are satisfied with. You may want to come back to this list from time to time to gauge your progress. As you work on yourself and make some of the changes you want to make, your list will look different. It's kind of like peeling an onion. As we begin to make positive changes, we find more things we want to work on. We are constantly growing and evolving toward a better life.

3

Taking Responsibility

Now that you have taken your personal inventory, the next step in creating the life you want is taking responsibility for your "stuff," that is, whatever baggage you're still carrying around with you.

All you need is to listen to any group of people talking, and you immediately realize we live in a society built on blaming outside forces for the conditions in our lives. We point to the government, our bosses, our spouses, our education, the economy, the school system, and, the ever-popular dumping ground, our dysfunctional families. We point to everyone but ourselves.

The problem with this kind of attitude is that it completely takes away our personal power to make changes.

Think about it. If the cause of my unhappiness or lack of prosperity is something outside my control, then how can I possibly expect to change it? If I am broke because of something the government did, like not raising Social Security payments, then I am stuck being broke! I can blame the government all I want, but I still pay the price.

> Responsibility is the thing people dread most of all. Yet it is the one thing in the world that develops us, gives us manhood or womanhood fibre.
>
> — Frank Crane

But if I take complete responsibility for my problems, I then have the power to do something about them. This may sound like an oversimplification or a mere play on words, but it is a critical distinction. We are always 100 percent responsible for our lives. Whether or not we "caused" our problems in our conscious or subconscious minds is irrelevant. The fact is, these situations are present in our lives, and if we see that we somehow contributed to their being there, we are then empowered to change them.

If, for instance, you blame the fact that you don't have the kind of job you would like on your lack of education, then you are stuck right where you are. But if you accept responsibility for this lack of education, you can do something in the present to change it. You could go back to school, take a correspondence course, study on your own, and so forth. The point is that once you take responsibility, you are empowered to change. Author Louise Hay once stated, "The point of power is always in the present moment." At any given time, we can choose to change. It is good for us to recognize that while we may move forward and backward in the course of changing, at least

> *If it's to be, it's up to me.*

we do not remain "stuck" in the powerless position of blaming. Begin now to take responsibility for creating the life you want. As Wayne Dyer suggested, "Make your life a work of art in progress."

4

Willingness

If you talk to anyone who has overcome an addiction, you will learn that he or she first had to be willing to go to any lengths to get help. In some cases, this meant moving to another state, changing jobs, or, in extreme cases, leaving their families. Whatever it took, those who succeeded were *willing*.

While you may not have an addiction, no doubt there are some changes you wish to make. The key is *willingness*. This does not necessarily mean that you will have to take drastic steps, but it does mean that you must be willing to do whatever is necessary to change your life.

If, for instance, you want a new career or a better job, perhaps you must become willing to go back to school to get the necessary education. If you would like a better relationship with your family, you may have to be willing to become more flexible in your demands. If you want to be able to take walks on the beach and you live in Kansas, you must be willing to move or to accept a different type of experience to give you pleasure.

The following exercise will help you to think about what you want to change in your life. I have broken this process down into fours steps: Write down one or two things you want to change, then ask yourself what you must become willing to do, what you must become willing to learn, and what you must become willing to change to make these changes.

For now, you just need to be willing to complete this exercise!

EXERCISE

◆

Making Changes

Take out your journal and respond to the following:

1. Based on your personal inventory, list one or two changes you want to make in your life.

2. What are some of the things you can do — right now — to make these changes?

3. What must you learn to implement these changes?

4. What needs to change for you to progress? For example, what changes do you need to make in your daily routine? What lifestyle changes do you need to make?

5

Purpose: A Reason to Expend Energy

Many years ago I read a statement made by Benjamin Disraeli: "The secret of success is consistency of purpose." Since then, I've been amazed at how often I have seen the effectiveness of this attitude. Why, for instance, do people age differently? What keeps some people going strong, while others seem to have given up on life and are just waiting for it to be over? I am convinced the difference lies in having a purpose. We need a reason to get out of bed in the morning. We need something outside ourselves to keep us going.

There is a wonderful story about a priest who goes to his doctor because of stomach pains. The doctor informs

15

him he has a terminal illness and suggests that he go home and put his affairs in order, as he does not have long to live. Having done this, the priest decides to make his final pilgrimage a visit to a church in Mexico he had always wanted to see. As he is approaching the church, he sees a young boy running off with the poor box. Grabbing the youngster by the scruff of the neck, he demands to know why he is stealing from the church. The priest learns that the boy, and many of his friends, is an orphan and has no food. He had stolen the poor box, the boy says, to buy something to eat. The priest is very moved by the boy's story and goes off into the village to see the poor conditions for himself. To make a long story short, the priest is so moved by what he sees that he begins an orphanage, and today, twenty-five years later, he is still running it. He had found a reason to keep going. The following exercise is designed to help you gain a sense of your purpose. It will help you understand what's important in your life.

> *The secret of success is consistency of purpose.*
>
> — Benjamin Disraeli

EXERCISE

◆

What Is Your Purpose?

In your head, or perhaps in your journal, answer the following questions:

- What gets your juices going? What makes you want to jump out of bed in the morning?
- What is important to you?
- What would you like to be remembered for?
- What do you stand for?
- What would you defend with your life?

6

Keep On Keeping On

Coco Chanel began her life in abject poverty, being raised in an orphanage. She taught herself how to sew and went on to become the first woman fashion designer, changing the style of women's clothes from Victorian to casual in the process. Her perseverance in overcoming enormous odds resulted in her building a fashion empire. Today, some eighty years later, the Chanel brand remains one of the benchmarks of quality and style. Thomas Edison tried almost ten thousand times before he succeeded

> *Never, never, never, never give up.*
>
> — Winston Churchill

in creating the electric light. If he had given up, you would be reading this book by kerosene lamp!

The original business plan for what was to become Federal Express was given a failing grade on Fred Smith's college exam. And in their early days, the company was struggling so much that their employees cashed their paychecks at retail stores rather than at banks. This meant it would take longer for the money to clear, thereby giving FedEx more time to cover their payroll. Sylvester Stallone was turned down a thousand times by agents and was down to his last $600 before he found a company that would produce *Rocky*. The rest is history!

> *Don't quit before the miracle happens!*

To truly succeed requires total commitment to your goal. Too many people make the mistake of quitting when they're just short of success. Keep going, no matter what. If you really believe in what you are doing, give it all you've got, and don't give up. You will succeed.

There is actually no such thing as failure. Every action produces an outcome. It may not always be the outcome you are looking for, but it is an outcome nonetheless. If you monitor the results of your actions and keep correcting what is not working, you will eventually produce the outcome you are looking for.

Be persistent. Ray Kroc, the late founder of McDonald's,

put it best when he said, "Nothing in this world can take the place of persistence. Talent will not; nothing is more common than unsuccessful [people] with great talent. Genius will not. Unrewarded genius is almost a proverb. Education will not. The world is full of educated derelicts. Persistence, determination, and love are omnipotent."

7

Commitment

Once you have gained a sense of purpose, the one trait that will keep you going in the face of obstacles is your commitment to what you want to accomplish. With a strong commitment, you can overcome anything. Without it, you are doomed to fail.

A friend of mine left his job and started his own business. When he began, I asked him how he felt about his new challenge. "I'll give it six months," he replied, "and if it doesn't work, I'll get another job." As you may have already guessed, he went out of business in about four months. Fortunately, the story has a happy ending. Recently, he and his wife opened a new venture. This time when I asked him how he felt, he said, "Great." He told me they had everything on the line and were going to make it succeed. His level of commitment to the second business has enabled him to build a successful enterprise.

When things do not go the way you want, and that will certainly happen, your level of commitment is being tested. If your commitment is strong, you will get through whatever is going on. Whether you are in a new relationship, starting a business, or wanting to lose a few pounds, the same principle applies. You must be totally committed.

> *Concerning all acts of initiative and creation, there is one elementary truth — that the moment one definitely commits oneself, then Providence moves, too.*
> — Johann Wolfgang von Goethe

Suppose for a moment that you want to start your own business. With the changes in the global economy, this has become an increasingly popular practice. You must first get committed to success. In his classic book *Think and Grow Rich*, Napoleon Hill talks about "burning all your bridges." The reason he suggests you do this is that if you have no other choice, you will use all your resources to accomplish what you want. Be wary of the trap of fence-sitting, the downfall of many well-intentioned people. Of course, you want to do this intelligently. This does not mean telling your boss off because you've started a part-time business. As a matter of fact, it's a good idea never to close doors when it comes to people. Those relationships, if properly nurtured, can become your most valuable resource. Rather, it means going wholeheartedly into whatever you're committing to. You must be committed. Remember the story about my friend? When he finally got serious, he succeeded.

One way to increase your level of commitment is to ask yourself why you are making this change in the first place. What will you gain from it? What will you lose out on by not doing it? The following exercise is designed to help you become clear about your commitment.

EXERCISE

◆

What Motivates You?

Refer back to the "Making Changes" exercise above. Choose one or both of the changes you want to make and write down all you will gain by taking these actions.

Be sure to reach deep within your soul to come up with the things that motivate you the most. If you are starting your own business, perhaps it is because you want more time with your family or to be your own boss. If your goal is to lose weight, perhaps it is because you want to live longer or attract that special someone.

Write as many reasons as you can think of for committing to taking the necessary steps. Next write what you are giving up by not taking these steps now. Really get tough with yourself. The idea is to get truly committed to what you desire to accomplish. Think about what you are losing out on right now as well as what you will lose in the future if you do not get serious now.

8

Developing a Positive Attitude

A magazine once reported that 22 percent of its survey respondents said the economy was in the early stages of a depression. An equal number said they thought an economic recovery was under way. They're all right! To quote the late personal development pioneer Earl Nightingale, "The mind moves in the direction of your currently dominant thoughts."

If you do not believe me, try not to think of the color red. Think of anything but the color red. Do you see my point? You automatically followed your thoughts, even though you are trying not to.

If we are looking for a depression, we will find it. However, if we continually seek the positive and ask ourselves how we can improve a situation, we will, I am certain, discover the silver lining in the cloud. I am not asking you to deny that there are difficult situations, and I am not asking you to take my word on this. Try it! You will draw your own conclusions based on your own experience. Yes, there is depression and, yes, there is recovery. It is up to us to choose where we want to play the game.

> *Whether you think you can or you can't, you're right.*

Later we will discuss ways in which we can learn to focus more on the positive in our lives through the use of questions, but for now try this simple technique. The next time you are faced with a situation that can be perceived as either positive or negative, instead of asking, "Why me?" (or some equally disempowering question), refocus your attention and ask instead, "What's good about this?" or "What can I learn from this situation?" (Hint: Try writing down the answers that come and keeping a journal of them.) You will begin to realize that we are in control of what the events in our lives mean to us.

9

"As a Man Thinketh in His Heart, So Is He"

This idea from the Bible appears in writings that date as far back as the beginning of recorded history. The same message is repeated over and over through the centuries: "The destiny of man is in his own soul," Herodotus (fifth century B.C.); "Our life is what our thoughts make of it," Marcus Aurelius (121–180); "A man's what he thinks about all day long," Ralph Waldo Emerson (1803–1882); "A man is literally what he thinks," James Allen (1849–1925); "We are what we believe we are," Benjamin N. Cardozo (1870–1938); "Our self-image, strongly held, essentially determines what we become," Maxwell Maltz (1899–1975); "All the resources we need are in the mind," Theodore Roosevelt (1858–1919). "We are spiritual and mental beings and live from the inside out through our minds" Catherine Ponder.

Unless all the people quoted above were crazy, our self-talk, the constant internal dialog we have with ourselves all day long, has more of an effect on us than we realize. We are continually having a conversation in our heads and, depending on what we are telling ourselves, it can either help or hinder our growth.

Here's a typical scenario: You've waited a long time for that special evening. The dinner turned out great, and your date was quite impressed that you were such a good cook. Everything was perfect until you began to serve the dessert and proceeded to pour hot coffee all over your date's designer outfit. If you were able to "freeze-frame" this moment, you would probably hear a conversation in your head that went something like this: "You dope! How could you be so stupid? Can't you ever do anything right? See, they were right when they said you were useless. Why don't you just go out and jump off a tall building?"

If you are like most people, your internal dialog is likely to continue in this fashion. This steady stream of dialog has been referred to as your chatterbox, your self-talk, your robot, your editor, and a number of other names, all of which describe that constant, usually negative, chatter going on inside your head.

I like the term *thought talk* because it seems a more

accurate way of identifying what is actually happening. Thought talk is that internal conversation we sometimes mistakenly call thinking, when a more accurate description would be talking to ourselves. You cannot stop the internal dialog, but you can change what you are telling yourself. We all have these conversations with ourselves. The difference between people who have a healthy self-image and those who do not is that the former have learned to control their thought talk and use it for positive reinforcement. For instance, when you perform a task well, why not tell yourself you did well, congratulate yourself, and, by so doing, teach your mind to reinforce this desirable behavior? On the other hand, when you make a mistake, rather than beat yourself up about it, why not just see it as a mistake and nothing more? Affirm that you will do better next time, and move on.

Somehow, in growing into adulthood, we have developed an insane belief that we should do everything perfectly. That's nonsense! If you have a small child and he or she is learning to walk, how many chances will you give the child to succeed? After a couple of tries will you tell the child she is stupid and say, "Okay, that's enough. You'll just have to crawl for the rest of your life. I guess you just don't have what it takes to be a walker"? I doubt you would react in this manner. Let me ask you then, why do you do it with yourself? This type of disempowering behavior is another reason people fear trying new things.

Fear of failure is probably one of the biggest obstacles to human progress. Again, we have this idea that we must be perfect right from the start. Think about anything you know how to do. Were you born being able to do it? (not hardly). Somewhere along the way you had to learn. I'll bet you were not very good at first, but with practice, you improved. All the things we take for granted, like tying our shoes, riding a bicycle, and driving a car, were skills we had to be taught. Give yourself permission to make mistakes. You will anyway, so you might as well allow yourself to. In so doing, you gain the freedom to experiment with your life. The philosopher Herbert Otto once said, "Change and growth take place when a person risks himself [or herself] and dares to experiment with his [or her] own life."

If we hold an image of what we want clearly in our minds and focus on it regularly (that is, daily), we will "move in the direction of our dreams."

10

Put a Little Gratitude in Your Attitude

One of the ways to remain positive is to develop an attitude of gratitude about your life. Whatever your present situation is, there are things you can be grateful for. What about your physical and mental health? Your family and friends? Look around where you live. Consider your possessions, your job, all the things we tend to take for granted.

Gratitude is one of the major keys to happiness. If you are feeling grateful for what you have, you will be a happy person. On the other hand, if you are constantly focusing on what you do not have, you will be miserable most of the time.

Remember that what you think about tends to expand. If you spend your time thinking about how lucky you are and how grateful you feel, then those thoughts will expand as well. Take out your journal and write down all the things you are grateful for, and when you're feeling down, take the list out and read it. When you feel great, add to the list. If you can't find anything to be grateful for, go visit someone in a hospital or homeless shelter and compare your problems with theirs.

11

Look Where You Want to Go

I f you were to ask a race car driver how he is able to get through those tight places without hitting anything, what you would hear is, "Look where you want to go, not where you don't want to go." If you look at the wall, chances are you will hit it. We can use this metaphor in our lives as well. Focus on what you want in your life rather than on what you don't want.

All too often people spend most of their time and energy thinking about what they want to get rid of — or what they don't want: I want to lose ten pounds or I wish I didn't have these bills. Try instead to focus on what you do want. I was talking about this with a friend recently and learned that the way skydivers are able to "link up" midair is by looking into the eyes of the person with whom they want to connect. Their bodies then follow, and they automatically move toward each other.

I was thinking about this one day when our cat, Ming, came into my office. He likes to sit by the window ledge behind my desk and fantasize about catching a bird. I watched him as he began his ritual for getting to the window ledge. First, he sits looking intently at the top of my desk. It's like he is focusing on being there. He then jumps to the desktop, a distance twenty times his height, easily and effortlessly. I realized that this is the same principle in action. Advance confidently in the direction of your goals.

> *What we need is more people who specialize in the impossible.*
>
> — Theodore Roethke

This practice works whether your goal is to start a nonprofit organization or simply to jump to the top of a desk. The other element that cannot be overlooked, as was appropriately pointed out to me, is faith. Ming has faith and trusts that he will not fall flat on his face, and so should we!

12

Do It Now

Recently, while talking with a friend who expressed an interest in obtaining a master's degree in classical literature, she said, "Yeah but I'm too old. If I were younger, I'd go back and get my degree." It saddens me to hear such comments, especially in light of some of the facts below, compliments of the *University of California Berkeley Wellness Letter*:

Giuseppe Verdi composed his "Ave Maria" at age eighty-five.

Martha Graham performed until she was seventy-five and choreographed her one hundred and eightieth work at age ninety-five.

Michelangelo was carving the Rondanini Pietà six days before he died at eighty-nine.

Marion Hart, sportswoman and author, learned to fly at age fifty-four and made seven nonstop solo flights across the Atlantic, the last time in 1975 at age eighty-three.

> *For of all sad words,*
> *of tongues or pen,*
> *the saddest are these:*
> *It might have been.*
>
> — John Greenleaf Whittier

Grandma Moses had her first one-woman show when she was eighty.

If you think you are too old to do something you've always wanted to do, you may want to reconsider and just go for it! Ask yourself, "What is the one thing I have always wanted to do but have been putting off?" Then ask, "If not now, when?" Write your cut-off date for doing it.

A woman once walked up to Wally (Famous) Amos after a talk he had given and remarked, "If I go to law school at my age I will be fifty-five when I graduate." Amos replied, "How old will you be if you don't go?"

13

Action

It is important to understand that whatever action you are now taking is producing a result. If you do not have what you want in your life it is because

> *Every action produces a result.*

the actions you are taking are producing the wrong results. For example, if you want to drop a few pounds and have actually gained weight, you have produced a result. It was just not the result you were looking for.

Following is a simple exercise to help you focus on your desired outcome and gauge the results of the actions you are taking.

EXERCISE

◆

Matching Actions to Outcome

Take out your journal.

First, list the outcome or result you want to achieve.

Second, ask yourself, What actions am I now taking toward this outcome? Write down your answer.

Next ask yourself, What is the result? Am I getting the results I want? If you are, great! If not, keep going.

Finally, ask yourself, How can I change or modify my actions to better reach my desired outcome? Record your answers.

14

Using Opposites
to Change How You Feel

If you change your thinking, you can change your life. In a similar fashion, if you change your focus, you will change your feelings. It's pretty simple, really. What you focus on will determine your emotional reaction and therefore the way you feel.

If you are like most of us, you will occasionally slip into self-pity. Some people spend most of their lives there. You've seen them. No matter what they have, they always find something to whine about. They always manage to focus on what is wrong rather than what is right in their lives.

Some see the glass as half-full, and some see it as half-empty. We choose how we view the world. You can take

39

control of your choices by employing a simple yet powerful concept called contrast. Using contrast is simply looking for references that are totally opposite of your current
thinking. For example, I love to sit on the beach and
write. One time I was writing while on vacation. We
were in Antigua at the St. James Club, a lovely, expensive
resort, complete with three restau-
rants, two beaches, and every
luxury you could imagine. This is
where movie stars and famous
people go to get away. It is mag-
nificent. I was writing about my
past experience. I was at a point
where I was describing in great detail what it was like to
be friendless, penniless, and hopeless. Lost in my writing,
I began to feel depressed. I stopped, looked up, and was
jolted back to the present. When I saw where I was and
considered how much my life had changed, a deep feeling of gratitude overcame me. When I realized how far I
had come, from being down and out to becoming a successful writer sitting on a beach in one of the world's most
luxurious resorts with a wonderful, loving wife, I saw I
had not a thing in the world to be sad about.

> *I felt bad because I had
> no shoes and then I saw
> a man who had no feet.*

Although I created this extreme contrast quite by
accident, you can intentionally do the same for any situation. If you are prone to bouts of self-pity or whining,
you can always find someone whose problems dwarf

yours. If you're complaining about something you do not have, go talk to a homeless person. That will help put things in perspective. You can also use contrast to motivate yourself to reach greater heights. It has been said that if you want to learn about wealth, hang out with people who are ten times wealthier than you are. If you want to motivate yourself to action, don't compare yourself to people who have less than you. It's too easy to slack off by saying, "I'm better off than him or her. I have a job and a home." That may make you feel good, but it won't help you grow. Instead, find people who have much more than you. Seek out people who have accomplished what you want to accomplish and use them as reference points.

15

My Ideal Day

Imagine that every day was perfect, that everything you did was exactly what you wanted to do, and that everything happened was according to your heart's desire. How would that make you feel? Pretty good, right?

Before you can expect your days to go according to plan, you must first develop an idea of what an ideal day would look like to you. In the following exercise, adapted from the book *You Can Have It All* by Arnold Patent, you are asked to design your perfect day. Think about the feelings associated with a day that you would consider perfect. Get out your journal and prepare to write about these feelings. As you write, pay particular attention to the feelings associated with your day rather than with actual activities. Of course, if there are certain activities you consider important, like walking in nature, then by all means list them. This exercise can be done daily. Soon you will establish a mind-set that will assist you in having great experiences.

EXERCISE

◆

Designing the Perfect Day

How does your job make you feel (ideally)?

See yourself happily interacting with the other people you encounter in your daily activities. As you write, see and feel yourself having wonderful experiences. Feel the joy in all your encounters and the pleasure you receive throughout your day.

Rather than focusing on a particular activity, consider the result of this activity. How do you feel when you engage in it? The actual activities can vary. The good feelings are what you are looking for.

The more often you perform this little exercise, the more control you will begin to have in your daily life and the more the quality of your experiences will improve.

16

Carpe Diem

How many times have you said, "I wish I had _____ (fill in the blank)"? How many of us have always wanted to do something new but hesitated because of a fear of failing or, worse yet, of not doing it perfectly?

> Remember:
> *Fear is only false emotion appearing real.*

Maybe you've always wanted to change careers, go back to school, or learn to play the clarinet. Perhaps it's something more physical like jumping out of an airplane or learning to play tennis. What are you waiting for?

The only thing stopping most of us is the fear that we

might fail. But is failing any more debilitating than sitting in a rocker twenty or thirty years from now and wondering what could have been if only you had taken a chance? Just go out and do it! One of the things stopping us is the quality of questions we ask ourselves.

All too often we ask poor questions like, "What if I fail, what if it doesn't work?" Instead, why not ask, "What if I succeed?" You may be pleasantly surprised by your answers.

> *The truth that many people never understand, until it is too late, is that the more you try to avoid suffering the more you suffer because smaller and more insignificant things begin to torture you in proportion to your fear of being hurt.*
>
> — Thomas Merton

EXERCISE

◆

What do I Fear?

In your journal, answer the following questions:
  What do I fear doing?
  What is the worst that can happen?
  What is the likelihood of that happening?
  What am I missing out on by not doing it?
  What will I get if I do take this action?
Do it now!

17

Go For It!

We experience whatever we hold consistently in our thoughts. Many people spend their waking moments thinking about what they do not want rather than what they do want. I believe, and statistics bear me out, that one of our major problems is that we do not set concrete goals. How can you expect to achieve anything if you do not know what you want? If you don't know where you're going, how are you going to know when you get there?

We spend more time planning our vacations than we do designing our lives. Think about it. If you are going to take a vacation, you do not just show up at the airport and ask if there are any planes leaving, do you? Nor do you get in your car and start driving with no destination in mind, right? Then why make any less effort in deciding where you want to go in your life?

You may have heard of the Yale University Study that took place in the 1950s. A survey of the graduating class revealed that only 3 percent of the group had written down their goals. A follow-up twenty years later found that those 3 percent had a net worth greater than the other 97 percent combined! I am not suggesting that money is the only measure of success, but I'm sure you see my point.

> *Ask and it will be given to you; seek and you will find; knock and the door will be opened to you.*
>
> — Matthew 7:7

One of my mentors, Anthony Robbins, reminds me that we generally overestimate what we can accomplish in a year but greatly underestimate what we can accomplish in a decade.

Rather than merely making some powerless New Year's resolutions, which you may break anyway, why not get serious about what you really want to have in your life?

18

The Why of Goals

There are a lot of wonderful books and tapes that teach you how to set goals, what kinds of goals you should consider, even how to write them down and what kind of paper to use. Yet they overlook a very important ingredient — namely, why! *Why* do you want to accomplish a particular goal in the first place? Understanding this is one of the keys to achieving a goal.

You may want to work for yourself, as so many people are doing these days. Okay, that's a reasonable desire. However, you will surely work harder toward achieving that goal if you have some strong reasons for wanting to be self-employed. For example, you may want to have more time to spend with your family. That kind of motivation gives you a better focus and increases your likelihood of reaching the goal.

The more you focus on your "why's," the more likely you will be to achieve your desires. You can accomplish any goal if you have a big enough why.

19

What Do You Really Want?

If you were to ask most people what they want, they would probably say "more money" or "to be happy." The only thing wrong with these desires is that they are too vague. More money could mean anything from five dollars in the hands of a homeless person to millions of dollars for a billionaire. What amount do you want? Similarly, being happy is not concrete enough. What would make you happy?

As I've said, people often talk about what they don't want. I hear things like, "I don't want all these lousy bills," or "I don't want to be fat." The problem here is that your mind does not work on the reverse of an idea. The more you focus on your bills, the more likely you are to have bills. The law of attraction states that whatever you focus on, you draw to you. As in magnetism, like attracts like. By holding your attention to something, whether it is desirable or undesirable, you will attract more of it toward you. Rather than focusing your attention on your bills, focus on the abundance you already have in your life. Noted author and teacher Louise Hay suggests "loving your bills" because they represent other's faith in your ability to pay. Making this simple shift in attitude can work wonders toward achieving financial freedom and a better state of mind about money.

As I said earlier, your mind moves in the direction of your dominant thoughts. The more detailed and clear your goals, the better your chances of attaining them. Spend some time now thinking about what you would like your life to be like.

If you have done goal setting before and feel you do not need the following exercise, please humor me and do it anyway. You may find that some of your goals have changed. Personally, I rework my goals about every three months. My life is constantly changing and improving, and my desires change along with everything else. Also, this gives me a way to measure how many of my goals I have already achieved. Unless you already have every single thing you want and your life is perfect, you can benefit from the simple exercises in the next few sections.

EXERCISE

◆

Dream Big

Please set aside a half hour to an hour or more for the exercise that follows. Find a quiet place where you will not be disturbed. Have your journal and a pen at hand.

I am going to ask you to forget for a moment that you are a reasonable, logical adult. I want you to think like a child. Pretend you are five or six again and it is Christmas. You are talking to Santa Claus and telling him everything you want. Dream big. Norman Vincent Peale once said that if you want a great life you need great dreams.

Let your logical mind take a nap for now and just allow your imagination to run wild. Children have no trouble setting huge goals. Ask a five-year-old what she wants, and she will probably say something like, "Disney World." Now is your chance to become childlike for a while.

Let's begin with material goals. For the next ten to fifteen minutes, write down what you desire. Do you want a new car? An airplane? A boat? Do you want to travel to faraway places? Swim with dolphins? Own a country house?

Write as fast as you can. There is no need for

detail right now. Just write down your main ideas. Do not edit yourself. Never mind for now how you will obtain these things. Just write down what you want. Do this for no more than fifteen minutes.

Next, we'll focus on your personal development goals. What do you want your life to be like? What about your physical condition and health? What skills would you like to learn? Would you like to learn a foreign language? Go back to school? Would you like to learn martial arts? Or how to meditate?

Now onto financial goals. How much money would you like to have in one year? In five years? Ten years? How much would you like to save? Spend another fifteen minutes on these answers.

20

Time Frames and Goals

In this next series of exercises, you will be asked to assign a realistic time frame for achieving your goals. For example, if you are just starting back to work after being on welfare, a goal of owning your own home is quite reasonable; however, doing it in one year's time may not be achievable. Perhaps a goal like that would be better on your "five-year" goals list. You will then write your reasons for wanting this goal in the first place. It is the "why" of our goals that drives us. Many people think they want money as a goal when, in fact, what they really want is what the money will do for them.

EXERCISE

◆

The When and Why of Your Goals

Now that you have brainstormed about your goals in life, assign a time for their completion. Break them down into one-year, five-year, and ten-year goals. Now select the most important one-year goal in each of the three categories and write them in your journal. Next write a short paragraph about why you will achieve these goals. Remember: If you have a big enough "why," you can achieve anything.

Write all the reasons you will not quit. Then write all you will gain by accomplishing these goals and all you will lose by not following through. Really get leverage on yourself. This is what will motivate you to take the actions necessary to create the life you want.

You may also want to write these things on a separate sheet of paper (or copy that page from your journal) and keep it with you. Refer to your goals often. Some people suggest reading them aloud each morning and night. What's important is that you stay focused on your goals and their achievement.

As you read your goals and keep them foremost

in your mind, you will begin to take actions toward their accomplishment. You will recognize opportunities that you hadn't noticed before. Events will seem to just "happen," and doors will open. There is magic in the practice of goal setting. Don't just take my word for it; try it for yourself!

21

Treasure Mapping

Now you have a clearly written list of your main goals. Once you have written down your goals, you further increase your likelihood of achieving them by using a technique called "Treasure Mapping."

A treasure map is simply a visual aid to help you stay focused on your goals. The more of your senses you can engage the better. Treasure maps are a powerful technique because they provide pictures for your subconscious mind to work with.

EXERCISE

◆

Making a Treasure Map

Using a piece of poster board, begin to build a map of your goal(s). If one of your goals is to lose weight, you may want to clip pictures of people who look the way you want to look and attach them to the board. A picture of yourself at the weight you want to attain would be even better, or you could paste your face on the picture of a person you would like to look like. These pictures and any other visual aids will help your subconscious absorb the idea. The more pictures and visual elements you can include the better.

You can make treasure maps of material goals by cutting out pictures and making a collage of the things you want. If, for instance, you want a new car, go to the dealer and obtain a picture of the make and model you want. Place this on your treasure map.

When you have finished, hang your map in a place where you will see it regularly. As you achieve your goals and set new ones, you can change your map. You can also make smaller treasure maps and carry them with you.

22

The Power of Affirmations

Affirmations are positive statements, usually written or spoken, that affirm what you want. They serve to condition your subconscious mind to what you specifically want to have or become. For example, an affirmation I used to help me quit smoking was *"I now release the need for cigarettes."* I would write and recite this periodically throughout the day, sometimes a hundred times. After a period of time, I found myself thinking more and more about quitting and, after being a very heavy smoker, I have not had a cigarette for twelve years. Affirmations are powerful ways to shift your thinking and begin to move you toward more desirable habits and beliefs.

Affirmations work for many reasons. The act of writing them down, as the following exercise will ask you to do, brings more than just your subconscious mind into play; it involves your body and nervous system. A friend of mine is a graphologist and graphotherapist, someone who uses handwriting analysis to analyze a person's tendencies and help him or her make changes. She uses handwriting exercises to help people deal with stressful situations. One of her patients was afraid of flying, so she created a simple handwriting exercise for the person to use while on a plane. The fact that exercises like these work leads me to believe there is a mind-body connection, which may explain the success of writing affirmations.

Actually, I do not know, or especially care, exactly how or why affirmations work. I just know they do. You too will find that writing affirmations is one of the greatest techniques in your arsenal of success strategies. I challenge you to do the following simple exercise for thirty days. You'll be pleased with the result. You don't have to take my word for it. See for yourself the power of this simple act.

EXERCISE

◆

Writing Your Affirmations

Develop one or two affirmations that express your desire or goal. Be sure they are in the present tense and positive. Use phrases such as *I am, I have, I own, I earn,* and so on. If you are currently working on making more money or managing it better, the following affirmation, taken from the book *Money Love* by Jerry Gillis, is a great one to use: "A lot more money is flowing into my life. I deserve it and use it for good for myself and others."

If your present challenge is health, you could write: "Each day I become healthier and healthier. I am physically fit and vibrant."

You can create short affirmations for any area you want to work on. Write them in your journal each day. I suggest writing them twenty-five times or more each day. You could easily write affirmations one hundred times a day by spreading the task out throughout the day. When you're on the telephone on hold, instead of sitting there doodling, write your affirmations.

Take a moment now to create one simple affirmation to help you move toward one of your important goals. Write it out slowly and deliberately in your journal. Next write it several more times. Do this daily for thirty days and notice what happens. If you make a practice of doing this daily, you will begin moving in the direction of your goals. I'd enjoy hearing about your experiences with this exercise. Please e-mail me with your story at jim@jimdonovan.com.

23

One Small Step

Carlos Casteneda writes, "A [person] of knowledge lives by acting, not by thinking about acting." Tony Robbins uses the metaphor "Knowledge is potential — action is power." I ask, "What is the difference between someone with ideas and someone who has successfully realized his or her ideas?" The only difference is the latter has taken action. This is the key to accomplishing anything in your life.

Make the extra phone call, write that extra letter, do whatever it is that you have a tendency to avoid doing. Procrastination is surely a death rattle. It will stop us from ever achieving our goals, from ever accomplishing what we want in our lives. It will prevent us from ever having what we want for ourselves and our loved ones. To live fully, you must end procrastination — now. Don't be like the person who was going to start a club for procrastinators but decided to wait.

How many times have you had a great idea for a business or an invention and six months later saw it sitting on a shelf somewhere? Someone had stolen your idea. How many times have you had an idea at work and hesitated, only to find that someone else had made the suggestion and received the credit for it? Let me ask you a question. What was the difference between you and the person who actually implemented your idea? I'm sure you have already guessed it. They took action. It's that simple.

> *If you want to pick the fruit, you have to go out on the limb.*
>
> — Shirley MacLaine

The way to realize your power and potential is to take action.

24

Getting into Action

One of the great incentives for continuing to set goals is having successfully accomplished one or two of the goals you have already set. When we reach a goal, it gives us a sense of fulfillment and encourages us to work toward even greater goals.

EXERCISE

◆

Assigning Immediate Action Steps

A good way to begin this practice of setting goals and taking concentrated action toward their achievement is to single out four or five areas of your life and assign specific action steps. For instance, if one of your main goals is to be in better health (something most of us would like to do), an action step could be to begin taking a daily walk. You could achieve this right now! You could put this book down and go out the door, take a walk, and come back to this later. Go ahead, I'll wait.

If one of your goals is to get a better job, perhaps you could call your local college or adult education center and request a catalog of courses. If you want to make more sales, you can start by making that extra phone call or going to see that hard to close prospect. Look at your goals list and, in your journal, write each main goal you have set. These can be short-term or even daily goals. Next to each, write one step you can take — right now — that will bring you closer to reaching that goal. For example, under "Goal" write "Get in shape." Under "Action Done," write "took a walk."

You get the general idea. What is important here is that you take action immediately! Later you can come back to this list and add additional action items as you progress.

25

Make Decisions Quickly

I have often found that making a decision, any decision at all, is better than sitting on the fence. When you are faced with a decision, gather all the information you can about the situation, weigh it carefully, sit quietly, get centered, and pray for guidance. Then act. Make a decision.

Don't be one of those people who are always thinking about what to do. We've all known them. These are the ones who spend endless hours going back and forth with every decision they encounter. They suffer the "paralysis of analysis." These are the people who, when presented with a business or investment opportunity, mull it over for so long that by the time they do decide, if ever, it's too late and the opportunity has passed them by.

At a young age, Microsoft founder and billionaire Bill Gates was faced with a decision that would shape his life and change the world in the process. While he was a student at Harvard, Gates saw the developing opportunity in personal computers. However, he was just a student. He also knew that time was a critical factor. If he waited too long, the window of opportunity would slam shut, and he would have missed his chance. Being the leader he is, he made a quick decision. He decided it was "now or never" and left Harvard, much to the dismay of his family, I'd imagine. The rest is history.

Not all decisions are of this magnitude. However, if you study successful people, you will discover that they all share this characteristic. They make decisions quickly and rarely change their position once they have decided.

You will make mistakes. You will occasionally make the wrong choice. This is normal. Making mistakes is one way we learn and grow. I've learned as much from bad decisions as I have from good ones. The more you use your decision-making abilities, the more you will learn to trust your inner voice, and the more you will fine-tune your decision-making skills.

I'm not suggesting you make snap judgments. By all means, gather all the information you need to make an intelligent decision. Pray for guidance. Listen to your inner voice. Then, when you've done your homework, make up your mind and take action.

Don't agonize over every move you make, sitting on the fence while the world passes you by. Decide, and act on your decision. Learn to listen to your inner guidance and trust your own judgment.

26

Results, Flexibility, and Role Models

Previously you developed an action plan for making changes in your life. Now let's discuss the details of monitoring your results, being flexible, and using role models.

The AA definition of insanity is doing the same thing over and over and expecting a different outcome. If you are taking action and not getting the results you are looking for — change your action! I realize this sounds like an oversimplification, but most of us fall into this trap. Out of habit, we continue to do things that are not working.

How many times have you misplaced your glasses or car keys? First, you look in all the usual places. Then, you look elsewhere. When you have still not found them, how many times have you gone back and looked in the same places again? Come on, let's get real. Did you think they would magically appear there? We have all done something like this at one time or another. We continue to take actions that do not produce the results we want. This makes no sense. If you do something and it does not work, do something else!

When he was asked about his "failures" Thomas Edison replied, "I have not failed, I have found thousands of ways that will not produce electric light. I am that much closer to discovering one that will."

That brings us to the second part. Be flexible! If an action is not working, change your approach. If you continue to take action, measure your results, and modify your actions, you will eventually reach your desired outcome.

I know this sounds tedious and time consuming. It can be. Fortunately, there is a shortcut called role modeling. Locate someone who has already accomplished what you are trying to accomplish. Find out exactly what he or she did. Ask what steps he or she took, then go out and do the same thing. Once, when I was trying to drop some weight by walking three days a week, I found it was not working. I talked to a friend who had lost weight and learned that he was successful because he walked seven days a week. When I did what he had done, I succeeded.

Go out and find role models, people who have successfully accomplished whatever it is you want to accomplish. If you want to learn about wealth, try this advice from Jim Rohn: "Take a millionaire to dinner." This may sound crazy, but think about it. Imagine what you can learn during a long dinner engagement. This is the least expensive financial consulting you will ever find.

27

The Power of Questions

If you can learn to formulate self-empowering questions and apply their answers, you can improve your situation and speed up your progress in any area of your life. This is perhaps the single most powerful strategy I have ever learned. Master it, and you will take control of your life. If you stop and think about it, we are constantly asking ourselves questions. What I am suggesting here is to consciously choose empowering questions rather than disempowering ones.

Too many people sabotage their progress and growth by asking what I like to refer to as "stupid questions." These are the closed-loop questions we ask ourselves. We ask things like, "Why me?" or "Why can't I lose weight, get a better job, get a date?" "Why can't I ever get along better with my parents?"

Asking this type of question establishes two conditions that undermine our well-being. First, we automatically establish that we are unable to do whatever it is we want to accomplish. Second, it just keeps our mind going around in circles looking for an answer. There is no answer to this type of question. That is the problem.

> *Ask and it will be given to you.*
>
> — Matthew 7:7

A more self-empowering approach would be to rephrase the question. "How can I spend time with my parents and have fun in the process?" Questions such as these, when used consistently, will cause our minds to seek solutions rather than go in circles. The Bible says, "Ask and it will be given," it does not say "whine"!

We are conditioned to answer questions. Do you agree? Do you disagree? Whatever your response, you had to ask yourself a question to determine your position. If someone asks you if you know the time, chances are you will answer him. It is human nature.

What I am suggesting is that we use this approach to assist us in our everyday lives. I have used this technique successfully many times. A word of caution: Be patient. If you keep asking positive, self-empowering questions, you will get answers. The following exercise will help you get started.

EXERCISE

◆

Asking Yourself Questions

Try asking yourself questions about a particular goal. For example, if, like so many people, you want to start your own business but do not know what kind, ask questions like, "What do I love to do?"

"What would I do if I knew I could not fail?"

"What would I do even if I were not paid for it?"

"How can I do that and make it profitable?"

You may be pleasantly surprised at the result.

In your journal, write one question to help you achieve a goal. As the answers come, write them down. You can even do this daily. Each day, ask the question and then spend a half hour or more writing the answers you receive. Over time, you will have collected a significant number of good ideas.

28

Questions to Start Your Day Off Right

I use a very powerful technique called Morning Questions. The following exercise explains how it works.

EXERCISE

◆

Morning Questions

When you first awaken in the morning and are in
bed or in the shower, ask yourself the following
questions and then answer them in your mind.

1. What am I grateful for today?
   What about that makes me grateful?
2. What am I excited about today?
   What about that excites me?
3. What am I happy about today?
   What about that makes me happy?
4. What am I committed to right now?
   What about that makes me feel committed?

By answering these simple questions, you will automatically direct your mind to positive thoughts. The obvious result is that you will feel better and begin your day in a better frame of mind. An added benefit of doing this simple exercise is that you will begin to look forward to waking up in the morning. You will have conditioned your mind to expect pleasant thoughts. Many people who are grumpy in the morning actually get that way as a result of asking "stupid questions" like, "Why do I have to get up so early?" Questions like this cannot help but put you in a bad mood. Morning questions will, on the other hand, increase your chances of having a good day by putting you in good mood first thing in the morning.

By using these and other questions you develop

yourself, you will experience major shifts in the way you feel and see positive changes occur in your life. I challenge you to do this for thirty days and see for yourself the difference it can make.

29

Become Curious

I f you really want to become more successful and live a full and exciting life, begin by becoming excited about life. Become interested in the people, places, and events you encounter daily.

Learn to become interested in other people and what they feel, think, and do. Every person you meet has a unique story or experience he or she would love to share with you, if you are interested in hearing it.

Most people are incredibly fascinating, if you will only take the time to learn who they are. At your job, make a habit of learning about your colleagues and associates.

Take time to learn what other people do in their jobs and how they do it.

Notice the world around you. It's so easy to take our lives for granted and not see them for the wonderful experiences they are or for the opportunities they present to us daily. By becoming more involved with the world around you, your life will become richer in every sense.

Get excited about life. Get in the game. Live, experience, see, and do new things. Get to know your fellow human beings. Make a point of leaving another person better off for having encountered you. Make a habit of doing these simple things, and you will begin to live a life that is more exciting and more enjoyable than you ever imagined.

If you are truly fortunate, you may hear that greatest of compliments: "It was nice talking with you."

> *We act as though comfort and luxury were the chief requirements of life, when all that we need to make us really happy is something to be enthusiastic about.*
>
> — Charles Kingsley

30

Choose Your Words Carefully

Our primary means of communication, with ourselves and with the outside world, is words, spoken and unspoken. We use words to interact with others as well as in our "self-talk" — the internal dialog we are constantly running in our heads.

Why then are we not more careful in our choice of the words we use?

A couple of years ago, I read an article about how we can use our vocabulary either to enhance or to weaken the effect of any experience. The concept is called "transformational vocabulary." This is really a fancy way of saying that, by changing the words we use to define a situation, we can change the effect it has on our lives. If you want to try out this technique, the next time someone asks you how you are feeling, instead of automatically reacting with "fine," try answering "great" and see how it makes you feel. Say it with enthusiasm and feeling.

We can change the words we use to increase the good feelings we want and, at the same time, reduce the effects of the not-so-good feelings. If, instead of saying, "She makes me really angry," you were to say something like, "I am a bit perturbed at her," it would change the effect the situation has on your emotions. With our words we can lighten the impact of the less-than-wonderful circumstances in our lives while greatly enhancing our good feelings. The next time someone asks, "How was your day?" instead of your usual "Okay," try saying "Fantastic" and notice how much better it feels. If you're feeling a bit under-the-weather, instead of saying, "I'm miserable, my head's stuffed, I can't breathe, I feel like I'm going to die any minute now," a response that is almost guaranteed to make you feel worse, you might just say, "I'm not quite myself today."

Rather than using negative terms to define people in your life, like your spouse, instead focus on their good points and use them when referring to the person. You may even notice their behavior change in a more positive direction as a result of your doing this. Words are powerful!

I should mention an additional benefit. It is called "fake it till you make it." I have noticed that when I answer "great" to the question, "How are you?" I feel better. Somehow the sound of the word *great,* as opposed to *fine,* makes me feel more upbeat. The reverse is also true. When I use less powerful words to describe negative feelings, it weakens their impact. Try this for the next few weeks and see for yourself.

31

Use Words That Work

Take a twenty-dollar bill and toss it on the floor. Now "try" to pick it up. You'll find that you can either pick it up or not pick it up. There is no such thing as *trying* to. *Try* is one of those self-sabotaging words we have made a part of our vocabulary. It is a weak word, one that we use to let ourselves off the hook when we know we will probably not do something. I'll try to be on time. I tried losing weight. I'll try to make it. These are all weak attempts at action. If you want results, change the word *try* to something more positive. I'll be on time. I'm planning to lose weight. I will be there. These words reflect a more positive intent and will be more likely to help you accomplish your objective.

It would be a good practice to eliminate the word *try* and other words that keep us stuck and prevent us from having all we deserve in our lives. Another word you will do well without is *can't*. There is a saying "If I can't, then I must." It would be wise to integrate this philosophy into your life. If you feel you can't do something, then perhaps that is the one thing keeping you from your dreams. Perhaps it is the one thing you must do.

For example, supposing you have just taken a job with a major hotel chain. You love everything about the job except the fact that you'll have to deal with unhappy or even angry people from time to time. You're great at everything else but you can't deal with irate people. If you want to succeed in your new career, tell yourself you *must* learn to deal with these people. You might take a course in "Dealing with Difficult People" or buy a book on the subject. Perhaps you can find someone on the job who successfully handles these situations and ask her to help you.

> *No! Try not! Do or do not! There is no try.*
>
> — Yoda

Maybe, like many of us, you want to get in better shape physically but are hanging on to a belief that you *can't* find time to exercise. By changing *can't* to *must*, you put yourself in a position to succeed.

This simple technique of changing the operative word radically changes your chances for success in whatever you do. What must you do to have the kind of life you want?

32

Energy Pickup

It's three in the afternoon, and your usual midday slump is about to take over. Every day around this time you begin to feel tired, and your productivity drops. What can be done? Most of us have been conditioned to reach for a cup of coffee as a way to pick ourselves up.

If you, like a lot of people, are trying not to drink coffee or to eliminate stimulants in general, you might want to try an alternative approach. Rapid physical movement is a quick and healthful way to boost your energy level. That may sound strange to you, but try it! Just stand up and begin clapping your hands rapidly while breathing deeply. If conditions permit, take a brisk walk.

However you accomplish it, the aim is to raise your pulse rate. After a few minutes, you will feel more energized. Like everything else in this book, don't blindly take my word for it; try it for yourself. You may look silly to your co-workers, but you'll sure feel better!

33

Ready, Set, Breathe

When was the last time you took a really deep breath? If you are like most people, breathing is something you take for granted. We assume we are breathing correctly, but this is not necessarily the case. Most of us have a very shallow breathing pattern, which can add to our everyday stress. When we get anxious, we tend to take short, rapid breaths.

One way to relax under pressure is purposely to slow your breathing and take long, deep breaths. Some time ago, a friend taught me a breathing technique that has been very useful in increasing my energy levels. It is something I can do any time during the day if I feel a bit run down.

The technique itself is pretty simple and originally comes from yoga. If you are going to try this, please remember not to strain at any time and to stop if you feel dizzy or light-headed. It is not necessary to strain when doing this technique. Regular, sustained practice over time will benefit you more than trying to master this in your first session. Of course, if you are under the care of a medical practitioner, please consult with her or him before undertaking this or any other physical exercise.

EXERCISE

◆

Counting Your Breaths

1. Inhale for a count of five or six (if this is too much, use a shorter count).
2. Hold it for a count equal to four times the inhale count, then exhale for a count equal to twice the inhale count. For example, using five as your inhale, you would hold the breath for a count of twenty and exhale for a count of ten.

Like I said, do not strain. If this ratio is too strenuous (if you smoke or are not in great shape it may well be too much) you can use a ratio of one to two to one. In this case, you inhale for a count of, say, five hold for a count of ten, and exhale for a count of five. Either way, if you do five to ten repetitions two to three times a day, you will begin to feel the results in a short time.

In addition to helping you feel more energized, this type of breathing has a cleansing effect on your body. Deep breathing causes lymphatic fluid to move through your system, which helps to cleanse the cells. All in all, this is an excellent practice, which I'm sure you will enjoy.

34

Worry: Silent Killer

Some time ago, I had a firsthand experience of the pain of having a loved one in the hospital. One of the things I got out of this challenge was an incredible motivation to stay healthy! In light of that goal, one area we can reduce or eliminate is needless worry.

Consider the following excerpt from Earl Nightingale's tape about how much time we spend worrying about

- Things that never happen: 40 percent
- Past events that can never be changed: 30 percent
- Our health: 12 percent

- Miscellaneous things: 10 percent
- Legitimate concerns: 8 percent

A full 92 percent of the average person's worries take up valuable time, cause painful stress, even mental anguish, and are absolutely unnecessary. If we can eliminate, or at least reduce, the amount of time we spend worrying needlessly, we can significantly reduce the level of stress in our lives and thus improve our health.

> *God grant me the serenity to accept the things I cannot change, courage to change the things I can, and wisdom to know the difference.*

35

Take Charge
of Your Health

A revolution is taking place in the United States with regard to health care. No longer are we willing to sit idly by and follow "doctor's orders." I am not suggesting that you stop listening to your doctor; however, it is time you took an active role in looking after your health.

Learn to ask questions. Do not be afraid to ask for a second opinion. There are still medical practitioners who will not answer their patients' questions and, worse yet, patients who still go to these people. Where your health is concerned, you have a right to know. Make sure your medical practitioner takes the time to explain the problem, and make sure you are satisfied with the answers. If your doctor refuses to answer your questions to your satisfaction, get another doctor! While you may not have gone to medical school, it is your health that is in question; you should be treated with respect by medical people, and your intelligence should be recognized.

Do your own research. With the advent of the Internet, you have the capacity to learn as much as you want about any medical condition. If you don't know how to do this, go to your local library and ask for help. One caution: Be sure you know the source of any medical advice you find online.

We need to develop partnerships with our doctors. It is not fair to your doctor to make them fully responsible for your health. Doctors can only do what they do. It's up to you to carry out their suggestions and take an active role in maintaining your own well-being. Too many people go to their doctor and expect a "quick fix." This does not work. If you want to become healthier, you must begin to make healthier choices in your dietary choices and physical activities. If you're constantly tired, a condition all too common in our modern society, you may need to reevaluate your diet and lifestyle. It is an interesting fact that in the United States alone, billions of dollars are being spent each year on alternative medicine, much of it out-of-pocket expenses paid for by the individual. And this figure has been growing steadily for several years.

Clearly people are starting to take their medical care into their own hands.

Personally, I've always liked the idea of a "health team." I have several practitioners on my team, each with a different specialty. I choose to be the captain of my health team for, in the final analysis, it's my life and health, and I'm willing to take responsibility for it.

36

Plant Your Garden

There's a saying in the computer industry: G.I., G.O. — "garbage in, garbage out." It means that you get out of something exactly what you put in. This principle applies to our minds as well. Norman Vincent Peale, perhaps the most well-known proponent of positive thinking, has said that if you remove all the negative thoughts from your mind, you must put something back in their place. We simply cannot live in a mental vacuum. If we do not replace the negative thoughts with something positive, they will eventually return and we will slip back into our old negative thinking patterns.

As James Allen said in his book *As a Man Thinketh*, "A [person's] mind may be likened to a garden, which may be intelligently cultivated or allowed to run wild; but whether cultivated or neglected, it must and will, bring forth." If we want our lives to remain positively directed, we must continually plant positive thoughts, affirmations, and sayings. This is why I am constantly reading motivational material, listening to tapes in my car, using affirmations, and trying to associate with positive people in general.

> *If we did all the things we are capable of doing, we would literally astonish ourselves.*
>
> — Thomas A. Edison

I have found that the quality of my life improves in direct proportion to the amount of time I spend listening to or reading positive, uplifting material. Maybe one of the reasons I write is that I need to continually reaffirm these principles for myself. An old proverb says, "We teach best what we most need to learn." If that is the case with my writing, so be it. My desired outcome is that we all benefit and grow from sharing these ideas. As Wayne Dyer so beautifully puts it, "Everybody on the planet who is on the side of helping to improve the quality of life for all people is on my team." We are, in fact, a team. We need to surround ourselves with people who are equally committed to personal growth. It is important to develop a network or support group of like-minded people.

With all the negativity around, it is extremely important for those of us who are trying to focus on the good and to promote positive ideas to share our experience and thoughts. This is truly a "win-win" situation.

37

Stress and Attitude

Norman Vincent Peale once said that what happens to us is not nearly as important as how we react to what happens. We are going to have stress in our lives, period. If we had no stress, we would be in a box six feet under.

What is important, however, is whether or not we will allow the everyday stresses to cause us problems. Negative reaction to stress causes, among other things, a tightening of our blood vessels and has been linked to heart disease. Additionally, many studies have linked stress with a weakened immune system.

Some ways of reducing the negative effects of stress are engaging in regular exercise and spending quiet time either meditating or in deep relaxation. In a stressful situation try asking yourself, "How important will this be in ten years?" This will help you put the situation in its proper perspective. And, of course, learn to accept the things you cannot change and change the things you can.

38

The Still, Small Voice

Every culture and religion embraces the practice of meditation. People have used meditation as a means of self-discovery since the beginning of recorded time. Recently, however, more discoveries have been made about the benefits derived from this practice.

Beyond the metaphysical aspects of meditating, there is scientific evidence that the regular practice of meditation helps slow the aging process. One study measured a group of adults for three variables pertaining to biological age. They monitored blood pressure, acuteness of hearing, and near-point vision. All three steadily deteriorate as the body ages. What was discovered was that meditators, as a group, were significantly younger biologically than they were chronologically. The best score was gotten by a female patient who was fully twenty years younger than her chronological age. A backup study in England later calculated that each year of regular meditation takes off roughly one year of aging.

What happens when we meditate? For one thing, our blood pressure is lowered and our heart rate slows down. When we meditate, we go into the "alpha" state. This state is associated with "waking sleep," when our brain is producing waves in the alpha range (four to eight cycles per second) as opposed to our regular awake (beta) state of ten to fifteen cycles or more per second. In the alpha state, we feel calmer and more relaxed and our bodies work more efficiently. Our internal healing mechanism is activated, and our brain's ability to produce neurotransmitter activity is improved. These activities partially explain some of the claims made for meditation such as that it increases intelligence and boosts self-healing. It is, in reality, our mind and body working at their highest potential that is doing all this. This is part of our inherent "magical" ability.

The mechanics are that the two sides of our brain are working together. Usually, in our normal waking state, one side is dominant and is guiding our actions. This partially explains why sometimes we feel creative and want to write a poem or play music (right-brained activities), while at other times we would rather balance our checkbooks (a left-brained activity). It is desirable to have both brain hemispheres working together as much as possible. Then we are tapping our fullest potential. The regular practice of meditation encourages this "hemispheric synchronization," or balancing of both sides of the brain.

It is by quieting our minds and eliminating the mental "chatter" that we normally experience that we can begin to hear what is referred to as the "still small voice," that quiet within that may appear as an intuition or flash of insight. As an added benefit, the more we practice inducing this alpha state through meditation, the more our brain produces these frequencies on its own. This is one reason why meditation results in an overall reduction of stress.

While numerous books and tapes deal with the subject of meditation, and classes are available almost anywhere, below is a quite simple exercise that will produce essentially the same result.

EXERCISE

◆

Simple Meditation

Find a quiet place where you will not be disturbed for twenty or thirty minutes. Sit comfortably, either cross-legged on a pillow or upright in a comfortable chair. You do not need to be able to sit in a full lotus pose to meditate. You can even lie down, although you may fall asleep this way.

Just sit quietly and begin to watch your breath. You may want to have some soothing music playing in the background. There are many great classical and new age pieces available specifically designed to assist you in meditation.

As you sit, quietly watch your breath and think to yourself the word *one* on each out breath. Do not try to force your breathing or expect to be able to silence your mind. Just let your mind wander as it will, bringing it back to watching your breathing as you sit quietly. Over time, you will find it easier and easier to quiet your mind.

If this exercise interests you, taking a class is probably the best way to learn simple meditation techniques. Most adult education centers offer classes, as do yoga and metaphysical centers.

39

Feeling Down?
Look Up!

The next time you are feeling a little depressed, try looking up. That's right, look up. Reach your arms overhead and let your eyes follow. You may be surprised to find that it is impossible to stay depressed while looking up into the air. You see, looking upward engages our visual sensory files, that part of our mind that sees pictures. Depression is usually a result of something we are hearing us tell ourselves.

By switching our senses, we are able to change the way we feel. This can also be useful if you are trying to talk to a depressed person. If you stand above her eye level while speaking to her, it will cause her to have to look up to see you and will help lift her mood. Another surefire remedy for the blues is rapid physical movement. Get up and move around. Go for a walk, jog, or swim. Do something that will raise your pulse rate. The increased activity will help rid you of your depression.

Who controls your emotions? I think you will agree that we control our thoughts. You may also agree that our thoughts produce our feelings. How, then, do you explain feeling depressed and not knowing why? We choose to think the thought. The thought produces a feeling, and we believe the feeling to be real when, in fact, we created the whole thing in the first place. It's one thing to build castles in the sky and quite another to try and move into them!

40

One Life to Live

If you want your life to be more memorable and exciting, try the following: Every week do something that you will remember for the rest of your life. Can you imagine living like this? Can you imagine how many truly exciting things you will experience? If you can, then go out and do them!

In your journal, list some of the things you would like to experience that would be memorable.

> *Do not go where*
> *the path may lead;*
> *go instead where there is*
> *no path and leave a trail.*
>
> — Ralph Waldo Emerson

41

Do What You Love

How many of us have talents we would love to pursue but don't, fearing that we won't be able to earn a living from them? Instead, we stay in jobs we dislike and relegate ourselves to a life of boredom, waiting for the day we retire so we can do what we really love. How many times do you hear people say, "I wish I could spend my days doing such and such, but I have to make a living?" How many people do you know who work at jobs they hate but are afraid to leave the security, or imagined security, they get from the job?

I am fortunate. Many years ago, someone told me that the only security I would ever have is my own ability. That philosophy has served me well over the years. It has allowed me to take some chances and has prevented me from getting stuck in a dead-end job.

Fortunately or unfortunately, depending on your perspective, times are changing. The once-secure corporate career is now a thing of the past. We no longer have any guarantees when we take a position with a company. We are no longer employed "for life." Even in Japan, where lifetime employment used to be the norm, companies are changing their policies. This change could be viewed as a positive development helping us take a step toward reaching our potential and living as free human beings.

If you love what you are doing, you will do it well. Further, people will seek you out, and you will, as a result, succeed. Think about it. If you know an auto mechanic who really loves fixing cars, chances are he or she is very good at it. Wouldn't you want to bring your car to this person instead of to someone who hates working on cars?

By doing what you love, you automatically succeed.

42

Love What You Do

Regardless of how much you love your work, there will always be some parts of it you do not care for. Worse yet, you may be in a job that you dislike but need to endure, at least for now. How then do you remain happy doing work you do not like?

The secret is to use empowering questions, as we discussed earlier. Rather than asking "stupid" questions like, "Why do I have to work in this lousy place?" (actually, you don't — if you are willing to pay the price for leaving) or, "Why is my boss such a jerk?" You can rephrase these questions into ones that will make the job more bearable. For example, you might ask, "What parts of this job do I like?" or, even better, "What new skills do I need to acquire to obtain a different job with a better boss?"

Even if you are fortunate enough to be in business for yourself, there will be tasks you do not cherish but must perform anyway. Again, you can use positive questions such as, "How can I make these tasks more enjoyable?" For example, if you have a lot of telephone calls to return, why not use the cordless phone and sit outside on your patio? Many people are using laptop computers in order to have more freedom in choosing where to work. If your work lends itself to this type of freedom, a laptop is well worth the investment.

Another way to handle chores you dislike is to schedule them early in the morning, a time when you are more likely to get them done. As an added incentive, plan a break and give yourself a reward for completing the task. This will motivate you and make the task easier to accept.

If possible, delegate some of your less desirable tasks to someone better suited to them. Usually we dislike certain tasks because they are not our strong points, while we tend to embrace those jobs we are good at.

43

Yes, You Are
Creative

We are all capable of being creative. To say you are
not creative is to deny yourself the experience
and pleasure of creative activities. You may not
have tapped into your creative abilities as yet, but that
does not mean you do not have them.

One simple method of enhancing your creativity is to
change the way you approach everyday tasks. Your brain
likes challenge and responds better to change than to
routine. Try looking at a problem or situation from a different viewpoint and see what ideas you come up with.

Change your daily routines. For example, try taking a
different route to work. Brush your teeth with the other

hand, or change the order in which you do your morning routine. This will stimulate your creative juices, and you will be surprised at how easily creative ideas will begin to flow.

One wonderful and very powerful technique is to use writing as a creativity exercise. In her book *The Artist's Way*, author Julia Cameron uses a technique she calls "morning pages," which are what they sound like — pages you write first thing in the morning. She suggests writing three pages every day as a way of getting in touch with your true feelings. I have used this technique for some time now and find that it is a terrific way to tap into my creativity.

Remember not to judge your ideas. Just relax and let them flow!

44

Going with the Flow

I once heard someone say that the last thing he let go of had claw marks on it! Letting go seems to be a big lesson for many of us. We somehow develop a fear of simply allowing life just to happen. We worry about the bills, our health, our families, our jobs, our pets, the weather, the economy, death, taxes, and anything else that seems to need our worry.

I read an analogy in one of Stuart Wilde's books that I loved: When the lion in the jungle wakes up in the morning, he doesn't begin his day by worrying where his lunch is coming from. He just goes about his business and trusts that everything else will work out. In most cases, for the lion and for us, it does.

We create a lot of our frustration by trying to control the outcome of events. That is not our job any more than it's the lion's job to control the jungle. I have noticed for myself that when I stop trying to control other people or the outcome of events and, to paraphrase William Shakespeare, to become a player upon this stage of life and endeavor to play my part well, my life flows and everything seems to work out for the best.

> *Rule number 1 is:*
> *Don't sweat the*
> *small stuff.*
> *Rule number 2 is:*
> *It's all small stuff.*
> *And if you can't fight*
> *and you can't flee, flow.*
>
> — Richard Carlson

I am not suggesting that we just sit and hope for things to get better, nor am I implying that we should ignore our responsibilities. On the contrary, I believe we have our part to play in this theater of life.

It is important for us to define what we want for ourselves and to take action toward achieving our goals. The lion does this automatically, without much thought. Below is a simple exercise you can do right now to help you accomplish this.

EXERCISE

◆

Letting Go

1. *Know what you want* (in the lion's case, it's lunch). Decide what you want. Define it as clearly as you can. Write it down. Visualize it happening. Write and say affirmations about it. Do whatever you can to get clear and stay focused on what you want.

2. *Take action toward your goals.* (The lion roams through the jungle. He doesn't just sit and wait.) Do the legwork. Continue to take steps toward what you want in your life. Note: If the action you are taking is clearly not working, change it.

3. *Then let go and let God.* There is a Higher Power at work in your life. Surrender to it. Know that everything is always happening for your highest good. You do not need to try to "make things happen."

4. *Measure the results of your action.* Modify your approach until you get the results you are looking for.

While this exercise seems contradictory, it is not. I can know what I want and take action while still letting go of the outcome. My part is to know what I want and take the necessary action toward achieving it. But — and this is a big *but* — I must also keep in mind that the actual mechanics of how that is to occur are out of my hands and should not be my primary concern.

There is a saying, "God moves mountains, but remember to bring a shovel." Although we can't control the outcome, we still have an important part to play, and it is our responsibility to play it as best we can.

45

Problem Solving

Every businessperson will attest to the fact that 80 percent of her business comes from 20 percent of her customers This is known as the eighty-twenty rule, and it applies equally well to many other situations. For instance, take a look in your closet, and you may be surprised at how it is also true for your wardrobe; that is we tend to wear only 20 percent of our clothes. I'm not sure why. It just seems to work out this way. We can use the eighty-twenty rule in solving problems as well.

All too often, we apply the reverse of this rule. We spend 80 percent of our time defining and redefining the problem and only 20 percent on finding solutions. How many times have you been with a group of people that just sat around discussing a problem over and over? People seem to think that talking about their problems long enough will somehow magically solve them. Clearly, this is not the case.

Why not try it the other way around? Why not devote only 20 percent of your time and energy to defining the problem? Define it clearly. If you want, write it down; however, once you have it clearly defined, do not spend any more time on it. From this point on, you are going to solve it.

Focus only on possible solutions. Write relevant questions, ask others for help, try sleeping on it, do whatever it takes; just stay focused on the solution. You will be amazed at how much faster you can solve what were once insurmountable problems. Sometimes the best action is no action. Many problems simply need time to sort themselves out. Of course, you'll want to avoid slipping into procrastination. Setting a date to work on a problem in the near future will enable you to step back from the situation while still making sure you address it.

I know a woman who even writes her problem on a piece of paper, folds it up, and puts it in the freezer to be dealt with at a later date! You can also write the problem down and burn the paper as a way of letting go of it.

46

The Gift of Giving

Do you ever find yourself asking questions like, "Why should I give, asking nothing in return?" "Why should I give my hard-earned money to charities and churches?" There was a time when I did ask myself those questions. I no longer have to ask.

It is human nature to want to help our fellow beings. Consider something that Wayne Dyer once said: "The fact that we do not take anything with us when we leave this earth is a strong clue that we are here to give — not to take." Think about that for a while.

Besides the good feeling I get from helping and giving when I can, I have been in business long enough to realize that everything that goes out comes back. The old saying "what goes around, comes around" is really true. I have had enough instances of this in my life that I no longer question it or try to write it off as coincidence.

There have been times when I have done something to help another person, and a short while later, with no connection, my phone will ring and someone will want to hire my company for a project. This has happened time and time again. Sometimes it is a referral, sometimes not. I do not need to understand the magic of the universe, I just have to accept it. Of course, if you start out with the intent of doing good because you will get something in return, that's another story. That's called manipulation. It doesn't work.

> *We make a living by what we get, but we make a life by what we give.*
>
> — Norman MacEswan

The religious principle of "tithing" is basically the same idea as giving. Tithing is giving a percentage of your income (usually around 10 percent) to your church, temple, or wherever you feel you receive spiritual nourishment. It is written in the Bible (the only book I know of that has been on the best-seller list for more than two thousand years) that whatever we give will come back to us tenfold.

I was once asked if I knew how much money billionaire J. Paul Getty left when he died. When I said I did not know, my friend replied, "All of it." You see, we are taking nothing with us when we pass, except our good deeds. To me, this simple fact is proof that we are here to give and serve. Otherwise, as Dr. Dyer said, we would be able to "take it with us."

The message here is simple. If we try to help each other and give where and when we can, good things will happen. It is truly a win-win practice. If you look at very successful people, you will see that one of the things they have in common is that they all gave much more to humanity then they took.

One of my favorite examples of this kind of person is the late Jim Henson. Henson was the creator of and driving force behind the *Muppets* and the original voice for, among others characters, Kermit the Frog. In my opinion he was one of the most talented and creative people in modern times. I once had the opportunity to briefly meet him and have always admired what he stood for and gave to us all. His motivation was to entertain children and by doing so very creatively, he made a lot of money. The money he made was a by-product of his efforts — not the focus. I think this is an important distinction. If you look at history, you will see that people who started out looking to make a quick buck usually fail, while those that do what they love and wish to add to the good of their fellow human beings usually succeed.

To help you think about how you could give more, take a moment to do this exercise. If you're not sure where you might be of assistance, look around your community. You will find plenty of opportunities to help. There are certainly several nonprofit agencies that can use your assistance as well as national and international agencies that need help. The exercise below will help you focus on your specific talents and areas of interest and help you uncover ways you can give back to your community, city, country, or even the world.

EXERCISE

◆

Compassionate Action

Ask yourself the following questions, and see what answers come up:

What can I do to help?

What resources do I have that I can share?

What action can I take today that can make a difference?

(Remember, sometimes all it takes is a telephone call or a kind word to make a difference in someone's life).

47

Feel the Fear

What is it about us human beings that makes us so willing to stay in an unhealthy situation just because it is familiar to us? Why would we rather remain in a dead-end job, continue in a destructive relationship, or stay "stuck" in a lifestyle we dislike simply because we are in a comfort zone of familiarity? Why is our attitude so often "I may be stuck in the mud, but at least it's my mud"? Is our fear of change so strong that we are willing to allow our lives to slip quietly by rather than face our fears and make changes to improve our situation?

If you are tired of being stuck and are ready to "feel the fear and do it anyway," as the title of the popular book has it, you can begin by developing a new belief that change is good. If you look back over your life and examine those times when you were forced to make changes, you will find that, when all was said and done, the outcome was positive and your life was enriched by having made the change. The fear associated with venturing into the unknown, whether it be in a new job, a new relationship, a new city, or changes in your daily routine is perfectly normal and to be expected. But while it is normal to feel a certain amount of fear and apprehension when making changes, it is destructive to allow this fear to immobilize us, causing us to remain stuck in the status quo. We can instead use the fear and transform it into motivation to take positive action.

First, acknowledge the fear. Trying to deny it will not make it go away. Accept that you have the fear and then refocus on the benefits you will gain by making the change. You can make a written list of all the good you will receive by taking action. For example, if you are going back to school (an event that can stir up a lot of old fears), focus on the new friends you will make, what you will learn, and ultimately, how you will benefit by having increased your knowledge and skills. If you are moving to

> *It's a funny thing about life; if you refuse to accept anything but the best, you very often get it.*
>
> — W. Somerset Maugham

a new city, instead of just worrying about whether you'll make new friends or feeling bad about leaving your familiar surroundings, focus on the chance you now have to change old, self-defeating habits and instill new, more empowering ones. Change interrupts our daily patterns, which is perhaps one reason we fear it. Moving is the perfect time to develop new habits and institute new behaviors. By

> *Carpe diem:*
> *Seize the day!*

viewing this change as an opportunity, you can change the experience from one of fear and apprehension to one of joy and expectation. All this happens by simply changing the way you perceive the experience.

You can learn to transform your fear into power and harness that power to thrust you into a more exciting and challenging life.

48

Change
Your Mind

A reporter once asked Mother Teresa about her response to one of his questions. "Several months ago," he stated, "you said 'such and such' and now you are saying something completely different. How do you explain the change in your position?" The saintly woman looked kindly at the man, smiled, and said simply, "I changed my mind. I did not know then what I know now."

What a simple concept! How many of us carry around beliefs and opinions that no longer fit with who we are, simply because we have always believed them? How many times have you held onto a limiting belief, saying, "That's the way I have always felt"? We have been taught that being consistent and unchanging is a positive characteristic, whereas changing our mind is a shortcoming. We have all heard someone who is "stable or rock solid" described with respect, while someone who changes her opinions gets called "wishy-washy." I am challenging this concept. Sure, consistency is worth developing in

> *Give yourself permission to change your mind.*

certain aspects of our lives. Trustworthiness, honesty, reliability, and dependability are all attributes worth striving for; however, it makes absolutely no sense to hold on to beliefs and opinions that do not serve us in the present just because they were true for us in the past.

We are allowed to change our minds! As a matter of fact, if we do not change them, we are in for a real struggle. Perhaps one of the leading causes of frustration is the fact that, while we are led to believe that it is good to be consistent, the world we live in is in a state of constant change. Every part of our lives, our planet, and our bodies, for that matter, are in a constant state of flux, while human beings, by nature, tend to resist change.

Herein lies the problem! We resist change in an ever-changing world. Resisting change in the face of a constantly changing environment has to be the height of insanity. Considering the pace at which the world is changing, it is important to learn to embrace change in our own lives. Give yourself permission to change. Reevaluate your beliefs and opinions and see if they are still true for you in this period in your growth.

Remember the old adage: "When one door closes, another one opens." If you look back, I'm sure you will find this has been true throughout your life.

49

Ongoing
Personal Development

A ten-thousand-meter cross-country ski event is won by four-tenths of a second. A golf tournament, after seventy-two holes, is decided by a difference of one or two strokes. A basketball championship is determined by a single basket. In life, as in sports, success is not achieved by making huge strides but by making small incremental gains, sustained over a period of time. If you study the most successful people, you generally find that their success was the result not of luck but of their willingness to "go the extra mile."

The big winners in sales, for example, achieve their success (and high incomes) not so much by making a "killing" on a sale but by making just one more call, seeing just one more prospect, writing just one more letter, which results in just one more sale. This practice, sustained over time, makes them the top performers and top income earners.

> *Our self-image, strongly held, essentially determines what we become.*
>
> — Maxwell Maltz

People who have achieved mastery of any skill have not gotten there overnight, nor did they "magically" wake up one day possessing the new skill. The accomplished pianist did not all-of-a-sudden just know how to play a Mozart concerto. She spent many hours in practice and, only then, achieved mastery. She became more and more skilled, day by day, never quitting, until one day her efforts paid off and she was able to play the piece with grace and ease. This type of sustained program results in long-term success.

People who have succeeded in the entertainment field have done so by following their dream with undying commitment. Jack Canfield and Mark Victor Hansen, co-authors of the hugely successful *Chicken Soup for the Soul* series of books were turned down by more than thirty publishers before finding one who would publish their first book. They have since broken all sales records with their books.

Our society has been sold the idea of the "quick fix," the "overnight success," and "instant gratification." Unfortunately, these ideas do not work. They have resulted in alcohol and drug addiction, depression, overeating, low self-esteem, and a generally unhappy population.

To truly succeed, we must be willing to do whatever it takes. We must develop a commitment to stretch ourselves and to take small actions regularly. I would like to share with you a simple acronym, O.P.D. It stands for Ongoing Personal Development. Simply put, this technique suggests making small daily improvements in every area of your life. O.P.D. can be applied to your work, family, health, finances, relationships, spirituality, and on and on.

I challenge you to embrace this simple idea and incorporate it into your life. Be willing to "go the extra mile." Make that extra call. Walk that extra mile. Write just one more letter. Paint just one more picture. Practice that hard second movement just once more. When you feel down and want to quit, remember Rocky from the movie and his undying commitment to give it his all! I promise you that if you adopt this principle and make small daily improvements you will, in a short time, have benefited more than you could ever imagine. Decide today to make O.P.D. part of your philosophy of life.

50

Live
Your Dreams

One day, while I was speaking on the phone with a friend, the conversation turned to business. I began describing my new office to him. I was telling him about the wonderful, pastoral view and the quiet, peaceful setting when he exclaimed, "You're living my dream!" "No, Joe," I replied. "I'm living *my* dream."

Several years ago, long before we located to our current home, Georgia, my wife, and I were driving past a lovely group of shops and offices. We began going to the shops while visiting the area on weekend "getaways" or while house hunting. One day I mentioned to Georgia that when the time came for me to move my business from our home into an office, this is where I wanted it to be. I kept a clear picture of this in my mind's eye, and my thoughts became my reality.

We really do create our reality with what we choose to dwell on. Any thought (desirable or less than desirable), consistently held in one's mind and acted on with faith, will materialize in the physical world. I am not simply writing about this. I have seen this principle demonstrated in my life over and over again in the past several years. Clearly defined, written goals, acted on with certainty, will become reality. This is a universal law! I do not know how or why this works. I simply know that it does.

The most difficult part for most of us is deciding what we really want. Young children have no problem doing this. Ask a child what he wants, and he will hand you a list. For some reason, as adults, we forget how to do this. Perhaps it is because we have been told all along to "be realistic" and settle for what we have. The truth is, we can have whatever we want. Our Creator has put it all here for the asking. We begin by asking ourselves what we really want.

I have found two exercises particularly useful for getting focused on my goals. The first I learned from Zig Ziglar, the widely recognized master of goal setting and one of the most popular public speakers in the country. He suggests you begin by writing a "dream sheet." Simply write a list of everything you want to have, to be, and to do in your life. Do not judge. Let the dreams flow. If you want a big life, you need big dreams. Later you can go back and pick out the really important goals.

The second technique I learned from my friend Teri Lonier, author of the highly successful books *Working Solo* and *The Working Solo Sourcebook* for solo entrepreneurs. Teri suggests the following: Imagine it is five years from now. You enter a room and shake hands with yourself. What do you see? Who is this person? What do they do? What do they look like? What have they done?

Please use these and other techniques you know to help you get clear about what you want in your life. Begin now to design the life you want. My wish for you is that you will know the pleasure that comes from being able to truthfully say, "I am living my dreams."

51

Problems Are
Opportunities in Disguise

I f you asked a roomful of people to set their problems
down in the front of the room, and then asked them
to pick up whatever problem they'd like, chances are
they would take back their own.

This is because our problems are really gifts in dis-
guise. Whatever problem you may be facing, it holds a
gift for you within it. The challenge is that this gift reveals
itself only after you've worked through the problem.

Most of what we call problems are situations that are
present in our lives to teach us something, to move us to
a new, higher level of functioning. Does knowing this
make handling the situation any easier? No! We need
some strategies to help get us through whatever we're

facing. One great way to make facing a problem less stressful is to get rid of the word *problem*. Replace it with something that is less unnerving, like *challenge*. After all, everyone likes a challenge. While this may seem like merely a word game, remember that words are powerful. By changing the words we use, we change the psychological effect they have on us.

> *There is no such thing as a problem without a gift for you in its hands. You seek problems because you need their gifts.*
>
> — Richard Bach

I've been using a great exercise recently to help me handle a personal challenge. I originally learned it from Dr. Robert Schuller. It's so simple, it's beautiful. Essentially what you are doing here is brainstorming. You are challenging your subconscious mind to deliver a solution to you. Remember, our conscious and subconscious mind will always provide the answer. It's sometimes only a matter of becoming quiet and waiting for the inspiration.

EXERCISE

◆

Solutions List

On a sheet of paper or a page in your journal write the words Solutions List across the top. If you'd like, you can restate your problem/challenge underneath.

Now, down the left side of the page, number from one to ten. Sit quietly where you won't be disturbed for a while. Asking for guidance from God or your Higher Power, write ten creative things you can do to have a positive impact on your situation. Let your mind expand and your creativity soar. Listen to your inner guidance. Be patient and wait for the ideas to come. By the time you've finished this little exercise, you will most likely have uncovered several good ideas you can put to use right away to handle your challenge. Then you will see the gift that was there all along.

You may want to repeat this exercise several days in a row. Do it until you have enough ideas to handle your challenge. Then get busy.

52

Accept What Is

How many people do you know who go around saying things like, "If I had such-and-such, I would succeed," or "If only they would change, I would be a winner"?

If you saw the movie *Glen Gary Glen Ross* with Jack Lemmon and Alec Baldwin, you saw a great example of this kind of person. In the movie, Jack Lemmon plays a real estate salesperson on his way down. He and the entire sales force complain throughout the movie about the quality of the leads. "If we had better leads, I could sell more." It's not an uplifting film, to say the least, especially if you're in sales, but it does make my point.

I have had numerous sales positions and have even hired and trained sales forces. Everyone blames the leads, territory, or product for their lack of success. It's always fascinated me that you can take a super salesperson out of her territory and put her in the "worst area," and in a short time she will again be a star.

The reason is simple. Successful people do not make excuses. They do not complain. They accept a situation and take responsibility. They learn to accept life on life's terms. There's an old saying that still holds true today: "If life gives you lemons, make lemonade." The line from the Serenity Prayer, which we read in an earlier section, "God grant me the serenity to accept the things I cannot change," is fitting here. There will always be things you cannot change.

> *Accept the things you cannot change.*

You may be working in a job you dislike because you lack the skills necessary for your dream career. You cannot change the present situation, however, you can change whether or not you will remain in a dead-end job. Instead of wasting time complaining and berating yourself for your lack of training, do something about it. That's the second part of the Serenity Prayer — "courage to change the things I can." The last part—"Wisdom to know the difference" is the key. If you're in an abusive relationship, for example, the wisdom is in knowing the difference between *being* in an abusive relationship and *staying* stuck in one. You may not be able to change the relationship, but you can change the part you play in it. You can go from being a victim to taking control of your life and getting the help you need to change the situation.

If you want to have a happier and more successful life, learn to accept the things you cannot change. Focus your time and energy on taking action and doing something about those areas that you can change. Instead of wasting time complaining about things that are beyond your control, spend your time on what you can change. There will always be many things that are totally out of your control. Accept them and move on.

You can use the Serenity Prayer to help you handle difficult situations while you gain the wisdom to know the difference between what you can and cannot change.

53

Cultivating Creativity

Many years ago, I had an associate named Ernie. Ernie was ten years older than I and was what some would consider a bit strange. He would often make odd comments, but he was a great salesperson, so I humored him. Besides, I liked him. Looking back, I realize he had learned some basic principles I had yet to explore.

One day Ernie came into my office and sat cross-legged on my desk, as was his habit, and exclaimed, "I have a great idea." He went on to explain how, while eating his lunch in a nearby park, he was approached by a duck. This was routine for Ernie. Now, most of us in

143

Ernie's place would have assumed that the duck wanted some food. Not Ernie. To him, the duck came bearing a message. "I started talking with the duck," he recounted. "And he gave me this great idea." He would then pass the idea on to me. Generally, it was some new idea about how we could market a given product, or sometimes it was a breakthrough idea for a new program to help solve a major problem. Almost every time, Ernie's *duck* ideas were significant ones.

> *While we have the gift of life, it seems to me the only tragedy is to allow part of us to die — whether it is our spirit, our creativity, or our glorious uniqueness.*
>
> — Gilda Radner

At this stage of my life, I understand what Ernie was trying to teach me. His lesson was that creative ideas do not come in a linear fashion. I, for one, receive very few ideas while at my desk. Most of my creativity comes while walking in nature, sitting on the beach, or even driving in my car. Sometimes, I even get new ideas from a duck! Movie mogul Steven Spielberg has said that when he needs to come up with breakthrough ideas, he goes for long drives in his car. I hear too many people telling themselves they are not creative. Nonsense! We are all creative. We may be creative in different ways; some of us write, some of us paint, and some of us create wonderful dinners. It's all creativity. Just because you do not draw does not mean you're not creative.

We are born to create. The problem is that we have not been shown how, so we assume it's a gift that others possess but that we do not. If you want to learn how to tap into your creativity, you need to follow some simple guidelines. For one thing, you must realize that you cannot force creativity. It's something that flows, given the opportunity. Creativity comes from our right brain, the part of our brain that is visual and deals in abstract ideas. If you try to use your more logical left brain — the side you use to balance your checkbook — it will not work.

One of the easiest and best ways to stimulate your creativity is to disrupt your patterns. We all develop daily patterns that cause us to operate on "autopilot." If you disrupt the pattern, you will begin to stimulate the creative, right side of your brain. Even small changes, like putting your shoes on differently, will bring out more of your creativity.

Change your routines. If you usually work at a desk and find creative ideas a challenge, get up and take a walk. You could even sit in a different part of your office. The change in your viewpoint will cause you to see things differently and may spark new ideas. Long walks in nature are great for stimulating your creative juices, as are times of quiet reflection and meditation. Getting out of your natural surroundings opens you up to new stimuli and visual inputs. This is one of the reasons we generally feel recharged after a vacation.

You cannot be creative under stress. Stress and worry, which is tied to a future event, are left-brain functions, since they cause you to be out of the present moment. By learning to relax and let your mind wander, you allow your creative impulses to surface. You may even find yourself, as my friend Ernie did, getting your break-through idea from a duck.

54

Be True
to Your Word

Has this ever happened to you? You're with a business associate and you mention wanting to contact so-and-so, and your associate replies, "Oh, I have the number. I'll send it to you." Then he never does. I never thought much about this until my friend, Tom, remarked that I was one of the few people he knew who actually did what I said I was going to do. I've always taken it for granted that if I said I would do something, it meant that I intended to do it.

Whether it's providing an associate with a contact name, taking out the trash, or simply making a telephone call, if you said you'd do it, then do it! It's easier to do what you say you'll do than it is to come up with excuses later for why you did not follow through. If you make a habit of keeping your promises, you will begin to notice a change in the way people respond to you. You will soon gain a reputation for being someone who is true to her word, a characteristic in short supply these days. The fact that most people, for whatever reason, do not do as they say makes you the unique one. People will remember your consistency, and you will stand out from the crowd.

> *This above all:*
> *to thine own self be true,*
> *And it must follow,*
> *as the night the day,*
> *Thou canst not then*
> *be false to any man.*
>
> — William Shakespeare,
> *Hamlet*

The next time you offer to do something for someone, do it. Write the letter, make the call, send the card or book, visit people you say you will visit. Soon you will become one of those rare people who "walks their talk." When you come right down to it, your word is all you have. It's what really matters in the clinch. People who have had major setbacks have found it easier to bounce back if they had a reputation for being true to their word.

Make it a part of your nature to do what you say you will. You will find it quite amazing how favorably people will react to you. People will tend to forgive and forget your so-called failures, providing you held true to your word when the chips were down.

55

Send
Thank-You Notes

One sure way to become known as a caring person is to acknowledge the actions of others. When someone does something for you, do you send a thank-you note? Do you send notes of appreciation to your customers acknowledging their importance to you? What about your loved ones? Do you take time to let them know they're special to you?

We all want recognition. We all want to feel appreciated. A simple thank-you note or card will help people feel acknowledged.

In the business world study after study has confirmed that the single most motivating factor among employees is recognition. It's not money, it's not power or more vacation time. It's recognition — that simple act of taking the time to acknowledge someone for his or her value to the company, of saying, "I value you and recognize what you have done."

A thank-you note can make someone's day. My personal preference has always been a handwritten card or note. A brief handwritten word or two of appreciation to a valued customer, or a short thank-you to a colleague, can have a major impact on how you are perceived. Keep a supply of blank cards handy and send them every chance you get. You'll be amazed at how your colleagues, friends, and loved ones will react to this simple, inexpensive, yet caring and considerate gesture.

When I first met my wife, Georgia, I began sending her little cards for no particular reason, a practice I continue to this day. It still amazes me how much of an impact this simple little act has on her mood. The little cards always brighten her day and are always appreciated. If you want to be more successful, become known as someone who, as Hallmark says, "cares enough to send the very best." If you study successful people, you will generally learn that they became that way because they cared about others.

Think back to the last time you received a card saying, "Thanks for being my friend." How did it make you feel? I'll bet it made your day. Why not take a moment right now to do the same for someone else?

56

Be on Time

Have you ever noticed that some people are always late? Are you one of those people? With regard to punctuality, it seems that there are three kinds of people.

There are the people who are always early, arriving for dinner while you're still getting dressed. There are the people who are always late, almost to the point that you start to calculate their tardiness. These are the friends you tell to come to dinner a half hour before you actually want them there.

Then there are the people who are punctual. While lateness can be tolerated, even amusing, among friends, it is a deterrent in your business life. It shows a lack of respect for the other person's time and presents you as disorganized and unreliable. I remember once having a meeting with someone who wanted me to collaborate with him on a book that he wanted to publish. The man waltzed in an hour and a half late and commented, "Oh, am I late?" I think, without realizing it, I made a subconscious decision at that moment to pass on the deal. While I did not hold it against him, his tardiness and lack of concern about it did nothing to help our potential relationship.

Be on time. It's not hard to do. All you need do is allow yourself enough time to get where you're going. You will reap enormous benefits from being prompt. Your promptness communicates that you respect the other person's time. It sends a message that you are busy and that your time is valuable, and it demonstrates your organizational abilities. Here's a tip: I've noticed, over a period of years, that the more I affirm, "I am always on time," the more I am.

The next business meeting you go to, be punctual. While the other people may not express their satisfaction, you can be sure that they will have noticed the fact. While showing up a half hour late may be tolerated among friends, even though it's still inconsiderate, in business it is definitely not acceptable. If you want to be more considerate to your friends and more successful in business, wear a watch and use it.

57

Become a Complimenter

Remember the last time you were paid a sincere compliment? Remember how good it made you feel? Remember how you immediately wanted to do something in return for the person who complimented you?

Paying someone a sincere compliment is a great way to build a relationship or begin a conversation. It makes the other person feel important and acknowledges his or her individuality. We all need to feel acknowledged in this way. Compliments help reinforce our positive self-image. A compliment costs you nothing and can be the most rewarding gift you can give to another human being.

There's a wonderful story from one of the old-time sales trainers, Willie Gale, who was speaking about compliments to a group of salesmen back in the 1950s. One of the men in the group, a door-to-door salesman, asked Willie what he would do if he rang the doorbell and the woman who answered was all disheveled, dressed in a housecoat, looking absolutely awful. (Remember, this was the 1950s.) Willie responded, "I would just stand there and keep looking until I found something to compliment her on."

> The best portion of a
> good man's life is
> his little, nameless,
> unremembered acts of
> kindness and of love.
>
> — William Wordsworth

A compliment must be sincere. People see right through false ones. Many a clothing salesperson has lost me as a customer by trying to convince me something looked good on me when I knew instinctively that it did not. Had they been honest, I would probably have bought something else, but since they were just telling me what they thought I wanted to hear, I would usually leave the store and not return.

Make a habit of freely offering sincere compliments to people you encounter. This is so important, especially in our hurried, harried, and sometimes impersonal society. There will be times when the compliment a person receives from you, a total stranger, is the only nice comment they hear all day. You can make a person's day with a simple word of kindness, spoken with thoughtfulness and sincerity.

58

Do More
in Less Time

I want to share with you a simple technique for managing your time and being more productive. There are several stories about where this time-saving technique originally came from. One tells of a young man approaching Andrew Carnegie, the head of U.S. Steel, while another simply has a man talking to the C.E.O. of a big company some time in the distant past. In one version the man was paid $100,000 for his idea on how to be more productive.

Regardless of where it came from, the technique remains valid and is one of the most effective, simplest productivity tools we can use. Whether you use a sophisticated computer calendar program, a complex time-management system, a leather-bound handwritten day-planner, or a simple spiral notebook, the idea is the same.

EXERCISE

◆

Time Management

In your journal, list the five most important things you have to do today, and do nothing else until you complete them.

I realize that this sounds overly simple in our exceedingly complicated world, but before you dismiss the idea, try it out for two weeks. This simple technique has been used by high-level executives, entrepreneurs, and professionals for more than fifty years. They use it because it works.

One of the keys is that by listing five items instead of ten or twenty, you are really focusing your energy on what is truly important. If you eliminate distractions and do only the five items on your list, you will be directing your energy to the most important tasks. Rather than wasting your valuable time doing busy work, you will be doing what really matters in your life. Of course, if you complete your list early in the day, you can always write another one, or do other less important tasks.

59

Celebrate
Your Life

When was the last time you actually "stopped and smelled the roses?" When did you last stop what you were doing long enough to take in the magic of a sunset? How much of the magnificence of the world around you do you notice each day?

If you're like most people, you get caught up in your daily routines and don't always take the time to appreciate this glorious experience we call life. We all do it. We get in a rut and forget to notice the simple beauty of the world around us. A rapidly paced society is robbing us of the very stuff life is made of. Life is not about a destination, arriving, or making it. It's about the journey. It's about the process of living.

Once, when I was living in southern California, a place of incredible beauty, I had become so complacent, so jaded, that I stopped noticing the majestic sunsets and the beautiful sunny days. My attitude had become "Oh, yes, the sun is setting in the ocean. I saw that last week."

Can you imagine taking life so much for granted?

> *Eighty-five percent of life is just showing up.*
>
> — Woody Allen

We are born, and we will die. These are absolutes. There's no way around it. We cannot change or control that fact. We can, however, make the time between these two events, whether it is a long or short time, exciting and wonderful, or we can live a life of quiet desperation. The choice is ours.

Make a habit of appreciating the world around you. Take time out from your hectic schedule to see what's right in front of you. Watch children playing, birds flitting about the trees, flowers blooming, and, yes, the sun setting in the ocean, if you are fortunate enough to live near the ocean.

There is magic all around us. All we need do is stop and take notice. There is no charge for admission. You don't need any special equipment. The good Lord provides us with this incredible spectacle each day. All we have to do is show up for it.

60

Don't Apologize
for Your Success

Have you ever noticed that the people who go around saying things like, "I don't care about money," or, "Money is not important," are generally people who are broke, or near broke? It's usually the people whose financial lives are not working who will deny the importance of money.

Then there are those who have some twisted idea that poverty is somehow "noble." I know. There was a time when I felt that way. This attitude is self-deprecating and self-defeating. The truth is that poverty has never brought out the best in anyone, except perhaps certain holy people who choose it as a way of life. All you need to do is visit a poor part of town. What do you see? Are the people concerned with helping each other, or are there tough conditions and a high crime rate? Probably the latter.

Of course, there are always exceptions. I know many kind, caring people who happen to be poor, and there are people who choose to live and work in low-income areas to try to help. However, I have never seen poverty bring out the best in people. How could it? If you are concerned with your very survival, how can you be concerned with your fellow human beings?

Don't confuse being poor with being spiritual. There are just as many spiritual people who are successful, even rich, as there are poor ones. You can do a lot more to help your fellow human beings if you have the means and willingness to do so. Please don't misunderstand. I'm not suggesting that you should worship money or that it is of supreme importance. However, it does have its place. It is a tool, a means to an end. Like fire, it can be used to build or to destroy. There are many, many people who are doing a lot of good in this world because they have the financial ability to do it. Throughout history, philanthropists have given to society because they were able to. Many of our colleges and universities exist today as a result of the foundations created by their wealthy benefactors and successful alumni.

Don't apologize for your success. You deserve it, and you are earning it. You see, we can have all the wealth and abundance we want if we believe in it and are willing to do something to get it. God has created an abundant world for us in which to live. If you don't believe that, go count the number of trees in a forest or the flowers in the fields. We are surrounded by abundance.

When you do become successful, learn to enjoy it. Don't be like one multimillionaire I knew who ate in second-class restaurants because he was too stingy to go to a decent one. He had a pile of money, but had never learned to enjoy it. Those people give the wealthy a bad name. If you have produced wealth and success, follow Paul Newman's advice and "spread it around." Enjoy the lifestyle you can now afford. After all, what is all the work for in the first place?

Of course, it is wise and prudent to save for the future. But you will enjoy your financial success more and be that much more motivated to continue creating wealth if you are receiving pleasure from the money you earn.

In addition to enjoying the fruits of your labor, make a habit of giving back. One of the greatest feelings of personal satisfaction comes from being able to give to others, especially those who are less fortunate. There are many ways you can use your wealth to enrich your community, your spiritual community, and the people who need a helping hand. As I've said before, it is virtually impossible to give without receiving.

Many people have the attitude that they will tithe when they, themselves, have more. This is backward. If you follow the teachings of the great teachers throughout history, you will learn that the best time to begin tithing is when you yourself are in need. This opens the flow of good toward you. Besides, it's a lot easier to make a habit out of tithing if you begin with small amounts. The wealthier you are, the larger the amount of your tithe and the harder it is to write the check. If you doubt this, imagine how it feels to tithe 10 percent of $1,000. Easy enough, right? You just write a $100 check. Now, imagine tithing the same 10 percent, but this time imagine the amount to be $100,000. The check you'd be writing would then be $10,000. Which would you find easier to give away?

> *I've been rich
> and I've been poor.
> Believe me, rich is better.*
>
> — Mae West

61

Don't Let Your Possessions Own You

One trap to avoid is becoming a slave to your "things." Make sure you own your possessions, not the other way around. Some years ago, I was taught a wonderful lesson about nonattachment to material things that has helped me keep my life in perspective. I was invited to visit the home of my then-yoga teacher and his wife. Driving to their apartment, I tried to imagine what the home of a spiritually focused yogi would be like. I imagined sitting on orange crates in a sparse room with bare floors, eating a simple meal of brown rice and tofu.

When we arrived I was floored at what I encountered. Their home was in a beautiful garden apartment complex, complete with a swimming pool. I walked into a lovely, spacious apartment, carefully decorated with white deep-pile wall-to-wall carpeting, fine teak furnishings, a top-of-the-line stereo, and beautiful artwork and wall hangings. What I realized was that although they had all these beautiful things, they were not attached to them. They enjoyed their material possessions but remained centered in their values, and if it all disappeared one day, they would not be devastated by it. This lesson in nonattachment was a valuable one for me and enabled me to keep my sanity when I did, in fact, lose everything some years later. Something else I noticed there was that they did not have an overabundance of *things*. They seemed to have found a balance between living in simple luxury and accumulating material objects just for the sake of having them.

Let's face it. Most of us have way too much stuff. Our society has tried to condition us that "more is better" and we must "keep up with the Joneses." This is not true. We don't have to acquire more and more material possessions just because the advertisers tell us to. We can all make ourselves happier by learning small ways to simplify our lives. Learn to lighten up your surroundings and your life.

My wife, Georgia, and I have made a practice of going through each room in our home several times a year and really looking at what we have. We look at each item and ask ourselves if it is something that is still serving us and when we last used it or, in the case of clothing, last wore it. If we are not using something or if we no longer have a need for it, we sell it, give it away, or throw it out. Are you still keeping your prom dress or the suit you got married in, telling yourself it will fit someday? Let it go.

Every time I do this little exercise, I feel lighter and freer physically, mentally, and emotionally. An added benefit is the good feeling I get by being able to pass things on to people who need them or can make better use of them.

Don't let money and material things control your life. You control them. Enjoy them, but remain true to yourself and your core values.

62

Be a Friend

It has been said that you are fortunate if you can number your friends on the fingers of one hand. True friends are rare indeed. I'm talking about those loyal individuals who are there for you no matter what, the people who are there through thick and thin, not only during the good times.

One sure way you can be happier and more successful is to be a true friend to those you care about. Sometimes, all a person needs is for someone to just be there for her when she's going through a difficult time.

Our lives tend to run in cycles of ups and downs. During those low times you learn who your real friends are. It's easy to attract a lot of would-be friends when you're in the limelight. But it is the people who are there after the spotlight stops shining that really count.

By being one of those loyal, trusted, true-to-life friends for others, you are giving a priceless gift, one that will be remembered. Besides making you feel good at the time, being this kind of individual can bring you nothing but success. Remember, as we give, so shall we receive.

> *Wherever our life touches yours, we help or hinder; wherever your life touches ours, you make us stronger or weaker.*
>
> — Booker T. Washington

Conclusion

ongratulations! You are well on your way to a happier and more fulfilling life. If you've read this far, you've probably realized that lasting happiness and an exciting life are not so much a matter of learning some new idea or making some huge change as they are of the small changes we make in our attitudes and behaviors.

I offer you a challenge: Follow your dreams, wherever they may take you. If you will do the "legwork" and apply some of the techniques outlined in this book, you can have the kind of life you deserve. Don't stop here, though. Many excellent books, tapes, lectures, and seminars await you. Become a stalker of new ideas and self-development. Keep a journal of your ideas, goals, and feelings. It's a great way to track your progress.

Make a habit of reading something uplifting and inspirational each day. It is our daily actions that will create our experiences and shape our destiny. Most important, have fun. Be gentle with yourself. We do not have to be perfect. Lighten up! Learn to relax and wear life as a loose-fitting garment.

Whatever it is you are seeking, I wish you all the success in finding it. May you live the life you have always imagined. Be well, and God bless.

> *Child of God,*
> *You Were Created to*
> *Create the Good, the*
> *Holy, and the Beautiful.*
> *Do Not Forget This.*
>
> — *A Course in Miracles*

— Jim Donovan
Buckingham, Pennsylvania

Bibliography

Below is a selection of some of the books that have been personally helpful to me.

Allen, James. *As You Think*. (Novato, Calif.: New World Library, 1998).

Allen, Marc. *The Ten Percent Solution*. (Novato, Calif.: New World Library, 2002).

Bible, The

Bijan. *Absolutely Effortless Prosperity*. (Las Vegas, Nev.: Effortless Prosperity, Inc., 1997).

Bristol, Claude. *The Magic of Believing*. (New York: Simon & Schuster, 1948).

Cameron, Julia. *The Artist's Way*. (New York: Jeremy P. Tarcher, 1992).

Canfield, Jack, and Mark Victor Hansen. *The Aladdin Factor*. (New York: Berkley Publishing Group, 1995).

Canfield, Jack, Mark Victor Hansen, and Les Hewett. *The Power of Focus*. (Deerfield Beach, Fla.: Health Communications, 2000).

Chopra, Deepak. *How to Know God*. (New York: Harmony Books, 2000).

Dyer, Wayne. *There's a Spiritual Solution to Every Problem.* (New York: HarperCollins, 2001).

———. *Wisdom of the Ages: A Modern Master Brings Eternal Truth into Everyday Lives.* (New York: HarperCollins, 1998).

Foundation for Inner Peace. *A Course in Miracles.* (Tiburon, Calif.: Foundation for Inner Peace, 1975).

Fox, Emmett. *Power Through Constructive Thinking.* (New York: HarperCollins, 1932).

Garro, Barbara. *Grow Yourself a Life You'll Love.* (Allen, Tex.: Thomas More Publishing, 2000).

Gillis, Jerry. *Money Love.* (New York: Warner Books, 1978).

Gawain, Shakti. *Creative Visualization.* (Novato, Calif.: New World Library, 1978).

Hay, Louise. *You Can Heal Your Life.* (Carlsbad, Calif.: Hay House, 1984).

Hill, Napoleon. *Think and Grow Rich.* (New York: Fawcett Columbine, 1960).

Holmes, Lauren. *Peak Evolution: Beyond Peak Performance and Peak Experience.* (Lewes, Del.: Naturality.net, 2001).

Jampolsky, Gerald G. *Love Is Letting Go of Fear.* (Berkeley, Calif.: Celestial Arts, 1979).

Johnson, Spencer. *Who Moved My Cheese? An Amazing Way to Deal with Change in Your Work and in Your Life.* (New York: G.P. Putnam Sons, 1998).

Keller, Jeff. *Attitude Is Everything: Change Your Attitude... and You Change Your Life.* (Tampa, Fla.: INTI Publishing, 1999).

Kiyosaki, Robert. *Retire Young, Retire Rich.* (New York: Warner Books, 2002).

Levine, Terri. *Work Yourself Happy.* (Buckingham, Pa.: Lahaska Press, 2000).

MacLaine, Shirley. *Out on a Limb.* (New York: Bantam Doubleday, 1983).

Mandino, Og. *Spellbinder's Gift.* (New York: Ballantine Books, 1995).

———. *The Greatest Miracle in the World.* (New York: Bantam, 1988).

McDonald, John. *The Message of a Master: A Classic Tale of Wealth, Wisdom, & the Secret of Success.* (Novato, Calif.: New World Library, 1993).

Millman, Dan. *The Life You Were Born to Live: A Guide to Finding Your Life Purpose.* (Tiburon, Calif.: HJ Kramer, 1995).

Mitchell, Mary. *Class Acts: How Good Manners Create Good Relationships and Good Relationships Create Good Manners.* (New York: M. Evans & Co., 2002).

Orman, Suzy. *The Courage to be Rich: Creating a Life of Material and Spiritual Abundance.* (New York: Riverhead Books, 1999).

Patent, Arnold. *You Can Have it All.* (New York: Pocket Books, 1997).

Peale, Norman Vincent. *The Power of Positive Thinking.* (New York: Ballantine Books, 1996).

Ponder, Catherine. *The Prospering Power of Prayer.* (Marina del Ray, Calif.: DeVorss & Company, 1983).

———. *Open Your Mind to Prosperity.* (Marina del Ray, Calif.: DeVorss & Company, 1984).

Price, John Randolph. *The Abundance Book.* (Carlsbad, Calif.: Hay House, 1978).

Roazzi, Vincent. *Spirituality of Success: Getting Rich With Integrity.* (Dallas, Tex.: Brown Books, 2002).

Robbins, Anthony. *Awaken the Giant Within: How to Take Immediate Control of Your Mental, Emotional, Physical & Financial Destiny!* (New York: Summit Books, 1991).

Shinn, Florence Shovel. *The Game of Life and How to Play It.* (Woodstock, N.Y.: Beekman Publishers, Inc., 1999).

Tolle, Eckhart. *The Power of Now: A Guide to Spiritual Enlightenment.* (Novato, Calif.: New World Library, 1999).

Waitely, Dennis. *Seeds of Greatness: The Ten Best-Kept Secrets of Total Success.* (New York: Pocket Books, 1986).

———. *Psychology of Winning.* (New York: Berkley Publishing Group, 1992).

Wilkinson, Bruce. *Prayer of Jabez: Breaking Through to the Blessed Life.* (Sisters, Ore.: Multnomah Publishers, 2000).

Wright, Kurt. *Breaking the Rules, Removing the Obstacles to Effortless High Performance.* (Lone Tree, Colo.: CPM Publishing, 1998).

Zoglio, Suzanne. *Create a Life That Tickles Your Soul: Finding Peace, Passion, & Purpose.* (Doylestown, Pa.: Tower Hill Press, 1999).

Zukav, Gary. *The Seat of the Soul.* (New York: Simon & Schuster, 1999).

About the Author

For more than twenty-five years, Jim Donovan has worked with individuals, companies, and organizations to implement strategies for personal and professional growth. Jim is a frequent speaker to businesses, trade groups, and associations, and his seminars have benefited hundreds of audiences nationwide. His seminars inspire individuals to take charge of their lives, provide them with transformational ideas and strategies for their success, and inspire them to achieve peak performance.

Jim's coaching programs employ a proven step-by-step process that synthesizes some of the most effective information, tools, and methods from the fields of marketing, sales, quantum physics, and universal spirituality. They are uniquely designed to identify the strengths within an organization and build on them. His focus is on helping clients produce significant, explosive results and to take quantum leaps well beyond what is expected.

As an internationally recognized author, his books, including *This Is Your Life, Not a Dress Rehearsal*, proven principles for creating the life of your dreams; *Reclaim Your Life*, how to regain your happiness through challenging times; and *Manage I.T.*, for new and aspiring IT managers, co-authored with Joe Santana, have been translated into four languages and distributed worldwide.

Since 1991, he has published an internationally syndicated newsletter for personal and professional development, aimed at business executives, entrepreneurs, and individuals. Jim is a popular guest on radio talk shows and TV stations, and a regular member of the "brain trust" for the Small Business Advocate syndicated radio show. His articles regularly appear in newspapers and magazines as well as on the Internet.

Visit www.jimdonovan.com to sign up for a free subscription to the *Jim's Jems* e-zine for personal and professional growth. Published since 1991, *Jim's Jems* is read by people throughout the world.

New World Library is dedicated to publishing books
and audios that inspire and challenge us to improve
the quality of our lives and our world.

Our books and tapes are available
in bookstores everywhere.
For a catalog of our complete library
of fine books and cassettes, contact:

New World Library
14 Pamaron Way
Novato, CA 94949

Phone: (415) 884-2100
Fax: (415) 884-2199
Or call toll free (800) 972-6657
Catalog requests: Ext. 50
Ordering: Ext. 52

E-mail: escort@nwlib.com
www.newworldlibrary.com